JONAH

THE DEPTHS OF GOD'S GRACE

The Proclaim Commentary Series

THE PROCLAIM COMMENTARY SERIES

JONAH

THE DEPTHS OF GOD'S GRACE

OLD TESTAMENT
VOLUME 32

MATTHEW STEVEN BLACK

PROCLAIM PUBLISHERS

WENATCHEE, WASHINGTON

Jonah: The Depths of God's Grace (The Proclaim Commentary Series)
Copyright © 2022 by Matthew Black
ISBN: 978-1-954858-23-7 (Print Book)
         978-1-954858-24-4 (eBook)

Proclaim Publishers
PO Box 2082, Wenatchee, WA 98807
proclaimpublishers.com

Cover art: *Jonah in the Storm painting*

Notes: (1) Ancient quotations have been at times changed to the ESV as well as some archaic language updated, and additional phrases added for clarification. At times verse references (non-existent until recent times) have been interspersed as well to guide the modern reader. (2) We have done our best to be careful in footnoting. Due to the nature of the sermonic material, various items are quoted freely, and may not have proper footnoting. If any great error is noticed, please contact the publisher, and it will be remedied in whatever way is available to us.

First Printing, November 2022
Manufactured in the United States of America

Dedicated to Pastor Jose Salgado. Thank you for not running from God's call. Your compassionate example inspires everyone who knows you!

CONTENTS

ABBREVIATIONS

Common

cf – Latin "conferatur", compare, or see, or see also
ff – and following (pages or verses)
i.e. – Latin "id est", that is
e.g. – Latin "exempli gratia", for example

Books of the Bible

OLD TESTAMENT

Genesis	Gen	Esther	Est
Exodus	Exo	Job	Job
Leviticus	Lev	Psalms	Psa
Numbers	Num	Proverbs	Pro
Deuteronomy	Deut	Ecclesiastes	Ecc
Joshua	Josh	Song of Solomon	Song
Judges	Jdg	Isaiah	Isa
Ruth	Rth	Jeremiah	Jer
1 Samuel	1 Sam	Lamentations	Lam
2 Samuel	2 Sam	Ezekiel	Eze
1 Kings	1 Kgs	Daniel	Dan
2 Kings	2 Kgs	Hosea	Hos
1 Chronicles	1 Chr	Joel	Joel
2 Chronicles	2 Chr	Amos	Amos
Ezra	Ezr	Obadiah	Oba
Nehemiah	Neh	Jonah	Jonah

Micah	Mic	Haggai	Hag
Nahum	Nah	Zechariah	Zech
Habakkuk	Hab	Malachi	Mal
Zephaniah	Zeph		

NEW TESTAMENT

Matthew	Mt	Titus	Titus
Mark	Mk	Philemon	Phm
Luke	Lk	Hebrews	Heb
John	Jn	James	Jas
Acts	Acts	1 Peter	1 Pet
Romans	Rom	2 Peter	2 Pet
1 Corinthians	1 Cor	1 John	1 Jn
2 Corinthians	2 Cor	2 John	2 Jn
Galatians	Gal	3 John	3 Jn
Ephesians	Eph	Jude	Jud
Philippians	Phil	Revelation	Rev
Colossians	Col		
1 Thessalonians	1 Thess		
2 Thessalonians	2 Thess		
1 Timothy	1 Tim		
2 Timothy	2 Tim		

INTRODUCTION

For as Jonah became a sign to the people of Nineveh, so will the Son of Man be to this generation.
LUKE 11:30

The Lord called Jonah to go to the great Assyrian city of Nineveh to pronounce judgment upon it. Jonah attempted to escape the Lord's calling by sailing to Tarshish, which was probably in the western Mediterranean, in or near Spain. Eventually he obeyed the Lord and went to Nineveh, at the heart of the Assyrian Empire.

AUTHOR

The book is named after its main human character, Jonah, a prophet in the northern kingdom of Israel. The book is one of "the Twelve," the traditional Jewish title for the Minor Prophets.

We are not told who wrote the book or when it was written. The presence of details only Jonah would have known—such as his prayer in chapter 2—could imply it was written shortly after the events it narrates by Jonah himself (after his repentance?), or by a contemporary prophet who knew him.[1] I hold the traditional view that this prophecy was written by Jonah.

---

[1] Jay Sklar, "Jonah," in *Daniel–Malachi*, ed. Iain M. Duguid, James M. Hamilton Jr., and Jay Sklar, vol. VII, ESV Expository Commentary (Wheaton, IL: Crossway, 2018), 389.

DATE AND LOCATION

Jonah prophesied during the prosperous time of King Jeroboam II
of Israel (2 Kgs 14:23–28), around the eight century B.C. Jonah's immediate predecessors were Elijah and Elisha. Jonah's fellow contemporary prophets were Amos and Hosea (*cf* Hos 1:1; Amos 1:1); Isaiah
immediately follows them. During this time the Assyrians were occu-
pied with matters elsewhere in the empire, allowing Jeroboam II to
capture much of Syria for Israel. Prosperity in northern Israel was at
unprecedented levels.

Nineveh, according to Jonah, had a circumference that could be
walked in three days, so about sixty miles, which is more like a province
than a city. To clarify, Commenting on this passage C. F. Keil remarks,

> It follows that the four places formed a large composite city, a large
> range of towns, to which the name of the (well-known) great city of
> *Nineveh* was applied, in distinction from Nineveh in the more re-
> stricted sense, with which Nimrod probably connected the other
> three places so as to form one great capital, possibly also the chief for-
> tress of his kingdom on the Tigris.[2]

This means that the expression "the great city of Nineveh" may well
designate not only the walled city of Nineveh, but also the surrounding
region, so that it might be better translated, "Greater Nineveh." This
would coincide with God's great heart to not just save people in a particular city, but in the entire region.

MESSAGE

The central message of the book remains especially relevant. *Salvation comes from the Lord.* It is not the exclusive possession of any
one group,[3] but is offered to the whole world, as we see from the pagan
Ninevites. Anyone who repents can be saved. We also see that salvation
must be of the Lord, since the prophet Jonah is such a poor messen-

---

[2] Carl Friedrich Keil and Franz Delitzsch, *Commentary on the Old Testament*,
vol. 7 (Peabody, MA: Hendrickson, 1996), 227.The description 'great city' is used of
Nineveh only in Genesis and Jonah.
[3] Donald J. Wiseman, T. Desmond Alexander, and Bruce K. Waltke, *Obadiah,
Jonah and Micah: An Introduction and Commentary*, vol. 26, Tyndale Old Testament
Commentaries (Downers Grove, IL: InterVarsity Press, 1988), 51.

ger—first, running from God's call to preach to Nineveh, and then sulking, petulant and angry at God's mercy to the merciless Ninevites. The book of Jonah illustrates the New Testament truth that God so loved the world of sinners that he would go to any lengths to save them.

OUTLINE

The outline of the book of Jonah follows the theme of the Lord as a God of worldwide grace, mercy, and love who desires to save all people. Thus he rescues the sailors in chapter 1, Jonah in chapter 2, and the Ninevites in chapter 3. In sharp contrast is Jonah, who delights to experience the Lord's mercy and salvation for himself (ch 2) but does not want to share it with evil Gentiles (ch 4).[4]

TESTIMONY

I have been personally convicted at how I am like Jonah. So often as I have read the book of Jonah over and over, I have been shocked and scandalized by the prophet's self-righteous pride. In preparing this volume, I realized I am Jonah, and my shock at Jonah uncovers my participation in his sins of self-righteousness. My heart is much smaller than I had imagined, and this precious book enlarged it. God showed me my many comfort zones and the whales he has used to keep me from falling away from my dear Jesus. All I can say is thank you to the true author of the book of Jonah, the Holy Spirit. How I want to walk in the Spirit and not be like Jonah at the end of the book. He had a great resume of revival but a poor reputation of anger in his heart. Lord, keep me happy and holy in your Spirit, walking in your peace and joy! And may I continually preach the "sign of Jonah"—the death, burial, and resurrection of Jesus. It's the only that sign of the Savior (his person and work on the cross) that saves!

Matthew Steven Black
Elgin, Illinois
October 15, 2022

---

[4] Sklar, "Jonah," in *Daniel–Malachi*, 389.

1 | JONAH 1:1-5

RUNNING FROM GOD

Jonah rose to flee to Tarshish from the presence of the LORD.
He went down to Joppa and found a ship going to Tarshish.
So he paid the fare and went down into it, to go with them
to Tarshish, away from the presence of the LORD.
JONAH 1:3

God's plan for the gospel is worldwide. But God's people often are too comfortable to reach the world, so we run from God. This is true all the way back to the Old Testament, here in the book of Jonah. God has a plan for salvation since "salvation is of the LORD" (2:9). With the prophet Jonah, we come face to face with a leader who is comfortable preaching in place he is familiar and at ease. About the year 755 B.C. the "word of the LORD came to Jonah the son of Amittai" (1:1). We find Jonah so attached to his comfort, that he is willing to run and hide from the presence of God.

I heard of about a pastor who phoned the home of some recent visitors to his church, and a voice on the other end of the phone answered with a hushed whispered "Hello."

The pastor said, "Who is this?"

The whisperer said, "Jimmy."

The pastor asked, "How old are you, Jimmy?"

"Four."

"Well, Jimmy, can I please speak to your mom?"

"She's busy too."

"Well then, Jimmy, can I please speak to your dad?"

"He's busy."

"Jimmy, are there any other adults in your home?"

"The police."

"Can I speak to one of the police officers?"

"They're busy."

"Jimmy, who else is there?"

"Firemen."

"Well, Jimmy, can you put one of the firemen on the phone?"

"They're all busy."

"Jimmy, what are they all busy doing?"

"They're busy looking for me."

Like Jimmy, a lot of people in life are hiding. Jonah's not just hiding but running from God. Jonah's story begins with him running from God and ends with him arguing against God, which raises the interesting question of when his book was written. You can't write under the inspiration of the Holy Spirit when you are arguing with God, so I assume that Jonah wrote this book late in his life and that his account offers his mature reflection on the triumph of God's grace. Some people teach us by their example; Jonah teaches us by his confession.[5]

We are studying the book of Jonah, the story of the greatest missionary dropout, who God refused to allow to dropout.

Key Thought: It is possible for a Christian to become so comfortable with earthly comforts, that he becomes uncomfortable with God. We may run from God, but in his unrelenting love he will find us and make us useful.

Here was a man who had served God, been religious for years, but when the test came, though he could teach about God, it seems it had been a while since Jonah had experienced the reality of God in a meaningful way. He froze. He backslid. He fell badly.[6] His comforts choked his spiritual life.

---

[5] Colin S. Smith, *Jonah: Navigating a God-centered Life* (Ross-shire, Scotland: Christian Focus Publications, 2012), Kindle edition.

[6] Timothy J. Keller, *The Timothy Keller Sermon Archive* (New York City: Redeemer Presbyterian Church, 2013).

Jonah was so comfortable on earth, that he ran from God and his heavenly plan. Really Jonah 1:1-5 is the story of how comfortable Christianity can numb us and kill our Christian life.

Jonah 1:1-5 | Now the word of the LORD came to Jonah the son of Amittai, saying, **2** "Arise, go to Nineveh, that great city, and call out against it, for their evil has come up before me." **3** But Jonah rose to flee to Tarshish from the presence of the LORD. He went down to Joppa and found a ship going to Tarshish. So he paid the fare and went down into it, to go with them to Tarshish, away from the presence of the LORD. **4** But the LORD hurled a great wind upon the sea, and there was a mighty tempest on the sea, so that the ship threatened to break up. **5** Then the mariners were afraid, and each cried out to his god. And they hurled the cargo that was in the ship into the sea to lighten it for them. But Jonah had gone down into the inner part of the ship and had lain down and was fast asleep.

You can have the greatest prosperity and good doctrine, but if you are not experiencing the living God, you are going to a "whited sepulcher" like the walking dead. Why do we run from God?

WE'RE DEADENED BY EARTHLY EASE (1:1)

Jonah loved earthly ease more than heavenly blessing. Like Jonah, we are like the proverbial frog in the kettle. The frog jumps into the pan of water, and the fire is turned up so slowly that the frog doesn't notice it. Before he knows it, he's a fried frog, a dead frog. Today, Christians who live in the prosperity of the West have great doctrine. They've figured out good programs to bring people in. But where is the presence of God? They are like the walking dead. Like the frog, we've slowly warmed up to the world's ideas, the worlds ideals, and the world has us by the throat. We've become deadened by earthly ease and materialism.

The Ease of Comfort

Jonah 1:1-2 | Now the word of the LORD came to Jonah the son of Amittai, saying, **2** "Arise, go to Nineveh, that great city, and call out against it, for their evil has come up before me."

Jonah was a prophet to the northern kingdom of Israel during the early part of the eighth century B.C. (c. 786–746). He was now in the midst of his prophetic career. He was the most popular prophet of his day due to his consistently optimistic forecasts regarding the military successes of Jeroboam II.[7]

> *2 Kings 14:25, NLT* | Jeroboam II recovered the territories of Israel between Lebo-hamath and the Dead Sea, just as the LORD, the God of Israel, had promised through Jonah son of Amittai, the prophet from Gath-hepher.

Jonah had supported Jeroboam's aggressive military policy to extend the nation's power and influence. The original readers of the book of Jonah would have remembered him as intensely patriotic, a highly partisan nationalist. [8]

Jonah had no idea of how self-absorbed he had become until God disturbed his comfortable life. He was devoted to ministry and listened, as a prophet, to the voice of God. But while he was ministering to others, his own heart had grown cold and, when God called Jonah to something new, the hidden layers of his inner life were revealed.

Let's not be too hard on Jonah though. It does say that God's word came to him. He heard the word of the Lord. He may not have liked it, but he did hear it. God's children hear God, and that is a hopeful reality for born again people both Old and New Testament. It was also good that Jonah was offended by the Assyrians sin. Jonah and all Israel knew that the Assyrians sins had piled up to heaven. Their solution was for God to send judgment. God's solution was to send Jonah and give these Ninevites an opportunity for mercy. Jonah didn't have God's heart of compassion because he had been hardened by ease and self-righteousness. God help us when we lose the compassionate heart of God.

The Ease of Ministry Success

Born in a godly home, and raised with knowledge of the truth, Jonah quickly developed a love for God and a heart for ministry. People in his hometown of Gath Hepher (near Nazareth) enjoyed Jonah's preaching, and he soon established a sterling reputation as a much

---

[7] James E. Smith, *The Minor Prophets*, Old Testament Survey Series (Joplin, MO: College Press, 1994), 101.

[8] Leslie C. Allen, *The Books of Joel, Obadiah, Jonah, and Micah* (Grand Rapids, MI: Wm. B. Eerdmans, 1976), 202.

loved and deeply respected teacher of God's word. [9] Just one thing was missing. He had drifted in his relationship with God.

He couldn't tell at first. He was like a person with numb feet who stepped on a nail. He was blind about his own heart and spiritual state. His conscience was fine, even though he had become far from God.

Jonah numbed himself with the success syndrome. "Things are going well, so I must be right with God." This was one of the most prosperous times in northern Israel, and the boundaries of the promised land are being reestablished, far beyond the borders of Israel north into Syria, and all the way south to the Dead Sea. It's an unparalleled time of prosperity and expansion. But don't confuse prosperity for God's blessing.

Jonah's selfish, self-indulgent heart is laid bare. You can know God's word and be a prophet and be so comfortable that your soul is lean. The Bible says in Psalm 106:15 that God can "grant our request" of earthly comfort but also send "leanness" to our souls, like those who died in the wilderness. Jonah was living in a materialistic culture like you and I live in today in the West.

Jonah is a powerful and convicting book to study because of the place incomparable comfort and luxury and ease we are experiencing here in Western culture. We are like Israel of old, with their culture of comfort came a culture of immorality. As it was in the days of Jonah, so it is today. Paul says, "in the last days perilous times shall come" (2 Tim 3:1). We are in dangerous, perilous times for God's people. The love of money and comfort is choking people's spiritual lives. We are going to see today that comfortable Christians will run from God. You've been saved. You've started down that journey of sanctification, but you've become comfortable. You've stopped being careful. Your heart has dulled. You've become lukewarm, even backslidden.

The Call to Awake

This series in Jonah is a wakeup call for comfortable, sleepy Christians. Wake up! There's a Nineveh out there. You're here, and you are happy, but you don't care as much about the lost anymore. You've lost your passion for evangelism. Maybe you've been beaten down by life. And you have even become distrusting of God. You are stuffing your soul with earthly ease to try to quell the conviction of your conscience.

---

[9] Smith, *Jonah*, Kindle Edition.

Wherever you are today, this message is for you. This message is a path back to the fear of God, and the love of God.

Jonah is a book about the depths of God's grace for those who run from him. We need the heavenly blessing of God more than all earthly riches. We need grace upon grace! We need to be growing from one level of glory to the next.

We all know that Jonah is a book about God's prophet running away from the will of God— that's sin, and God chases after Jonah — that's grace. His grace is greater than your sin. What sin are you hiding? What sinful habit do you keep telling God, "I'll deal with it later"? Don't run from God. He wants to heal you. He wants to help you. Do you desire heaven's blessings more than earthly comfort? Let's consider another reason Jonah and all of us run from this amazing God we serve.

WE DRIFT FROM GOD'S PRESENCE (1:2)

We can become so familiar with a superficial knowledge of God that we take him for granted, and we drift from God's presence. Oh, how Jonah drifted, but he didn't even know it.

Jonah certainly was comfortable preaching to his crowds in Samaria. Jeroboam II must have been please as God was giving Jonah prophecies about the expansion of the northern kingdom that rivaled the times of Solomon. The main reason Jonah can try (unsuccessfully) to run away from the presence of God in his call, is because Jonah had already drifted away in his own heart.

We can become so insulated and self-righteous when everything is going so well. We forget about the lost and dying world because we embrace our own self-righteousness and drift from the love of God. Holiness is simply being set apart to know and love God. What we find out is that Jonah is a descent prophet, popular even. But he's drifted from knowing the heart of God. He's drifted because of passivity.

God tells Jonah to arise out of his comfort and go to the most nightmarish place he could ever imagine. Think of the worst person and the worst people imaginable. God wants to save them! There used to be a segment on a political show called "worst person in the world." Well, the worst group in the world for Jonah was the people of Nineveh, the capital city of the great Assyrian empire. Nineveh is modern day Mosul, Iraq, located along the Tigris River.

Don't Drift from God's Amazing Love

Doing God's will can be hard because of a self-righteous view of ourselves. Jonah thought he was more righteous and pure than God.

Jonah 1:1-3a | Now the word of the LORD came to Jonah the son of Amittai, saying, **2** "Arise, go to Nineveh, that great city, and call out against it, for their evil has come up before me." **3** But Jonah rose to flee to Tarshish from the presence of the LORD.

Of course, God is offended with evil. He is pure and holy and cannot dwell with evil. But God always acts in pursing love and grace toward the worst of sinners because of his covenant of grace through Jesus. The Lord enlists Jonah to "arise and go to Nineveh," around 550 miles northeast of Israel on land. God says to us: "Go into all the world, and preach the gospel to every creature," even the Ninevites. Jonah wants nothing to do with it! He hates the Ninevites. Because of this he has been called, "the world's worst missionary"!

God wants to save the people Jonah and Israel most feared. In Jonah's mind, he had good reason for fleeing. They were the most ruthless terrorist state in the ancient world the ISIS of the ancient world. [10] They were dreaded. They were like an army of the worst Nazis. They were worse than 9/11 hijackers. When you understand the tactics of the Assyrians, you understand a little more why he hated them. The Assyrians were so brutal in the way they handled their prisoners of war. They would torture women and children. They had such sophisticated torture that they made serial killers look tame.

Their torture was so fearful and ruthless that when people heard the Assyrians were coming, a whole town or village would just commit suicide. They would rather kill themselves than experience what was coming. That's how feared the Assyrian empire was; they were that dreaded and that hated. Even though Jonah is eventually going to bring a revival to Nineveh (circa 755 B.C.), not much more than thirty years later in 722 B.C., Assyria is going to destroy northern Israel so that they will never recover.

Barbaric Practices. You can read the barbarous practices of the Assyrians in history books. Records brag of live dismemberment, often leaving one hand attached so they could shake it before the person died.

---

[10] James Bruckner, *Jonah, Nahum, Habakkuk, Zephaniah*, The NIV Application Commentary (Grand Rapids, MI: Zondervan Publishing House, 2004), 28-30.

They forced friends and family members to parade with the decapitated heads of their loved ones elevated on poles. They pulled out prisoners' tongues and stretched their bodies with ropes so they could be flayed alive and their skins displayed on city walls. They burned adolescents alive.[11] Then once they were dead, they would behead them, and they would take the heads of all of the prisoners of war, and they would make a pyramid of heads outside their city to say to the rest of the world, "This is a city that we conquered."

Those who survived the destruction of their cities were fated to endure cruel and violent forms of slavery.[12] When you understand the depravity of these evil practices, maybe you have a little more mercy for Jonah when he says, "I don't want to go there. I hate these people."

It's almost certain that Jonah had a relative or a friend, or someone who'd actually experienced the horrific mayhem of the Assyrians. Jonah had good reason to despise the Assyrians. Yet God says, "I want you to go and bring them to repentance." In Jonah's mind, he had legitimate reasons why he didn't want to obey God. "I don't want to live in heaven with Assyrians forever." Or maybe he said, "There are some people God should just not forgive."

Yet it was this barbaric nation that was the object of God's missionary outreach and his unrelenting love.[13] God's lovingkindness and compassion and grace is not limited to good people, but to brutal, murderous, idolatrous pagans. The self-righteous and the self-indulgent all need Jesus.

Have you drifted from the amazement of the gospel? Paul as a self-righteous Pharisee had to be humbled to the dust. He declared his own unworthiness above all the wicked people of the earth, he was most wicked and most unworthy.

1 Timothy 1:15 | The saying is trustworthy and deserving of full acceptance, that Christ Jesus came into the world to save sinners, of whom I am the foremost.

---

[11] Ibid.

[12] Timothy Keller, *Rediscovering Jonah: The Secret to God's Mercy* (New York: Penguin Publishing Group, 2018), 11.

[13] Ibid.

Don't Drift from God's Amazing Power

We know that Jonah was given a call to preach in a pagan city. "The word of the Lord came to Jonah" (1:1), and he disobeyed the call of God because he knew God's power. He knew God could transform the hardest of sinners. And Jonah wanted nothing of it.

> **Jonah 1:2-3a** | Arise, go to Nineveh, that great city, and call out against it, for their evil has come up before me. **3** But Jonah rose to flee to Tarshish from the presence of the LORD.

Jonah was fine with the Assyrians dying and going to their eternal punishment. He didn't want to see them saved. He was uncomfortable with the idea of them coming into the kingdom of God.

What a history Nineveh had. The infamous Nimrod was the founder of Nineveh. Nineveh's ruler had called himself "the almighty." This was a city full of idols. God wanted to change their history, and he had the omnipotent power to do it. But he calls earthly messengers to bring heaven-sent, supernatural power. Nineveh means "fish city" and they worshipped Dagon, the fish god, like the Philistines. So God sends them a prophet that's literally going to be vomited out of a fish!

He was clear what he wanted Jonah to do. He wanted Jonah to go to this place that was way outside his comfort zone. Jonah was to call out against the people of Nineveh. The evil was so great, we have this picture of it piling so high it touched the heavens. God says, "their evil has come up before me" –the stench of their vile lives stank in the nostrils of God.

God's power is so great that he could bring the entire city of Nineveh to repentance. God can work in the hardest hearts! We know that Jonah was from a town called Gath-hepher near Nazareth where our Lord was later raised. Jesus mentions Jonah in Matthew 12. They repented in a greater way with Jonah's weak preaching than those who were eyewitnesses of Christ's ministry.

> *Matthew 12:41* | The men of Nineveh shall rise in judgment with this generation, and shall condemn it: because they repented at the preaching of Jonah; and, behold, a greater than Jonah *is* here.

Jonah was glad for the power of God to be displayed in Israel, but he was content to never see God work in places like Assyria. I'll tell you, God is all about getting us to a place where his power is at work among us and then in the most unlikely places and people!

Don't Drift from God's Amazing Plans

Jonah 1:3a | But Jonah rose to flee to Tarshish from the presence of the LORD.

God has amazing plans not just for you, but for the whole world. Jonah as a prophet was also a theologian. He knew he could never outrun the presence of God. Yet, as Peter would later confess, it is possible to drift away from God that you can forget everything you know about God.

2 Peter 2:9 | Whoever lacks these qualities [*of Christian growth*] is so nearsighted that he is blind, having forgotten that he was cleansed from his former sins.

Jonah had become so self-righteous and comfortable that he was angry with the mercy of God. When Jonah heard God's plan and ran as fast and as far as he could in the opposite direction! Jonah ran because he felt he had better plans than God. But God says:

Jeremiah 29:11 | For I know the plans I have for you," says the LORD. "They are plans for good and not for disaster, to give you a future and a hope.

Jonah doubted the goodness, wisdom, and justice of God. We have all had that experience. We sit in the doctor's office stunned by the biopsy report. We despair of ever finding decent employment after the last lead has dried up. We wonder why the family we had always dreamed of and hoped for—is not what we thought it would be. Maybe for some of you it has crashed and burned. It just seems like God doesn't know what he's doing.

Listen, you may have allowed circumstances to blind you. You desperately need to get your eyes back on the gracious, loving God who has plans to prosper you and see you conformed to Jesus Christ (Rom 8:29).

WE QUIT GOD'S CALL (1:3)

Have you ever tried to run from God? When trials and difficulty come, we have a temptation to escape to worldly distractions—easy outs. The smallest distraction can turn us into practical atheists, where our minds can escape from the thought of God and his call on our lives.

God has a call on every Christians life. You can try to run from it, but you cannot escape it. The sooner you open up the sewers of your flesh life and clean your heart by the power of the Spirit, the sooner you will see the power of God's call on your life.

Jonah needs a great fish to crush him. He comes out of that fish, covered in the acid of the fish's stomach, probably looking like an albino on the shores of Nineveh.

Quitting is Pointless

Don't resist God's call. You can't quit God's call. Peter tried. Moses tried. Elijah tried. You can't quit dear brother. Jonah tried to quit.

> **Jonah 1:3** | But Jonah rose to flee to Tarshish from the presence of the LORD. He went down to Joppa and found a ship going to Tarshish. So he paid the fare and went down into it, to go with them to Tarshish, away from the presence of the LORD.

We all know we can't escape physically by fleeing from the presence of God, the way Jonah did. But we're experts at quitting by ignoring the plain teaching of God's word, distracting ourselves with busyness, and offering alternative plans and rationalizations in place of full obedience. There are no offramps to sanctification for the Christian.

No matter how we rationalize and excuse ourselves, our rebellion leads only to pain and suffering. There are always plenty of boats sailing in the wrong direction. When God calls us to fulfill his plans and purposes for our lives, it is futile to run from God's call because he is everywhere. You can't outrun God. You can't quit God's call.

A walk to Joppa. What was Jonah's response to God's call? Jonah's response to the call is quite immediate and quite clear. Jonah runs from the call of the God of grace. Look at the *lengths* he goes to in order to *avoid* God's call! He's supposed to go 550 miles northwest to Ninevah (modern day Iraq). It says here in verse 3 that he goes in the opposite direction, "down to Joppa" (a Philistine seaport), and he pays his fare and gets on a boat and heads to Tarshish. Consider how far Jonah was willing to go to avoid the call of God. Jonah lives near Nazareth—a very short distance from the shores of the Sea of Galilee. He was willing to go by foot to Joppa, which is 50 miles away. Fifty miles by foot is the picture of a man who wants to get far away!

A boat ride to Spain! But that's just the beginning of his journey! Jonah wants to get on this boat and go to Tarshish. Tarshish is in modern day Spain, near the Rock of Gibraltar. That's around 2500 miles away on the opposite side of the Mediterranean Sea! Jonah wanted to go to the other side of the then known world. Jonah is running as far as he can run from God! In the map below you can see the lengths Jonah is willing to take to run from the presence of God. This was like the end of the earth for Jonah. It was so far and so costly to get there, it was likely he was never planning on returning to Israel. All this running was pointless. Who can run from the omnipresent God?

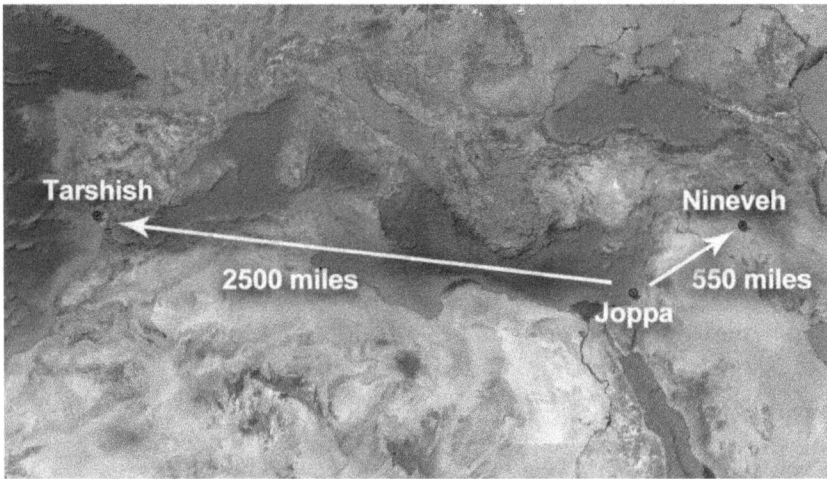

Quitting is Impossible

Jonah was turned around when he thought he could exit God's plan and his presence. He thought he could quit. He thought wrong.

Jonah 1:3a | But Jonah rose to flee to Tarshish from the presence of the LORD.

If God has called you, and you are a child of God, you can't quit until God is finished with you. Look at Jonah. He's so unwilling. So God sent a fish. How many fishes does God own? How many ways can God chase you down. If God wants you to do something, you can't contend with the power of the almighty over your life. You are predestined for holiness.

Romans 8:28-29 | We know that for those who love God all things work together for good, for those who are called according to his purpose. [29] For those whom he foreknew he also predestined to be conformed to the image of his Son.

This promise is rooted in the Abrahamic covenant. God promised to bless all nations through the Seed of Abraham, which is Christ. He doesn't depend on us to accomplish this covenant of grace. God's covenant with his people from the beginning is a monergistic covenant. Abraham was asleep when the Abrahamic covenant was cut. He was asleep for a reason. God was the only one that could perfectly keep the covenant.

You are going to fail, but God never fails. His plans always, always, always come to pass, and you are part of God's plan. So get this in your heart: you can't quit. God will chase you down. He can use a fish. For me he used a Ford F-350. It was a massive truck. It mowed me down in 2018. That was four years ago. I needed that truck! I praise God for that truck.

God twice reveals that Jonah's intention is to "flee from the presence of the LORD." When I think of the story of Jonah, I often think of the striking verses in Psalm 139. There is no where we can flee from God's presence.

Psalm 139:7-10 | Where shall I go from your Spirit? Or where shall I flee from your presence? [8] If I ascend to heaven, you are there! If I make my bed in Sheol, you are there! [9] If I take the wings of the morning and dwell in the uttermost parts of the sea, [10] even there your hand shall lead me, and your right hand shall hold me.

We are often as deluded as Jonah was! *We cannot run from God,* for he is *omnipresent!* The one thing you will never be able to do is *run from the presence of God.* Remember this. You may try to quit God's calling on your life, but as God's child, he's put his omnipotent Spirit inside of you.

Why did he sail for Tarshish? He was far from God. He was angry with God. He was sickened by God's plan. So he took a very long, long trip! One commentary said that **it** would take about a year to sail from where he was to where he was going. That's a lot of running.

You can take years off your life trying to run from God, but God's plan is to conform you to Christ! Your life is predestined to lead to your sanctification. You can't quit. You can't stop God's call on your life. You can try to exit, but every exit leads right back to God.

WE'RE ASLEEP IN GOD'S STORMS (1:4-5)

We know what happened. Jonah got on a boat. He went 3000 miles to Tarshish, near Gibraltar in Spain. It takes a year to get there. He's got a lot of time on his hands. Sometime in the journey, God sends a terrible storm, and Jonah's outer body matches his inner spirit. He is asleep. And truly Jonah was a sleepy, backslidden prophet. He had fallen away like the prodigal's son. And don't you know that God loves prodigals?

Backsliding Makes Us Sleepy

Jonah 1:4-5 | But the LORD hurled a great wind upon the sea, and there was a mighty tempest on the sea, so that the ship threatened to break up. **5** Then the mariners were afraid, and each cried out to his god. And they hurled the cargo that was in the ship into the sea to lighten it for them. But Jonah had gone down into the inner part of the ship and had lain down and was fast asleep.

Jonah's hatred for the Assyrians made him spiritual dead and sleepy. Jonah boards a year-long cruise to Tarshish in Spain, and somewhere along the way he sleeps. Trying times today can make us sleepy. The toxins of modern politics draw us in and deadens us with fear and hatred. Many Christians watch the news cycle much more than they read their Bibles or commune with God. This will make us sleepy! The apostle Paul said that "in the last days perilous times shall come" (2 Tim 3:1). I believe we are living in those perilous—dangerous—days. These are days of great uncertainty. We face uncertainty in the financial realms of our country. Corporate scandal and increased government programs are costly to everyone. We face uncertainty in the job and financial markets because of runaway inflation. We face concerns about terrorism and wars around the world. These are days of political and social unrest—not to mention moral unrest. The homosexual agenda is making inroads into the fabric of our society. There are still hundreds of abortion mills right here in our state of Illinois where babies are being murdered. We witness a continuing moral decline with a tidal wave of pornography sweeping away the strength of our nation's men and women—both young and old. Drug and alcohol use is increasing. Kids are dying of overdoses more now than any time in our history. The family unit continues to disintegrate. Divorce, adultery, premarital affairs, and unmarried couples living together are commonplace. Entertainment is increasingly laced with sensuality, violence, and materialism.[14] God calls his backsliding people to get out of the storm and return to him.

> *Jeremiah 3:22* | Return, faithless people; I will cure you of backsliding. "Yes, we will come to you, for you are the LORD our God."

God will bring whatever storm necessary to humble you, so you are fit for his love and his leading. God had to send a storm to Jonah in order to bring him back. Listen to your call, saint of God!

> *Ephesians 5:14* | Awake, O sleeper, and arise from the dead, and Christ will shine on you.

When I lived in Louisiana, I loved to go canoeing. Once I got in a canoe with my friend Chris. We were young kids, maybe 12 years old. He had made this canoe with fiberglass with his dad in his garage. And we got to talking. Then, we looked up, and I was like, "Where's your house?" It took a minute, but I had lost track of where we were. I didn't know where I was for a moment. We had drifted several houses down and we didn't even know it until we looked back at our point of reference. We hadn't realized just how far we had drifted.

Some of you, you may be able to relate, because maybe months or years ago, you were really close to God. You know what I'm talking about. You're praying and God answers your prayers. You walked with God. God would prompt you to do something or say something, and so you do it or say it and then, He'd bless you. And you were like: "Whoa, that's just amazing." His word was a valuable part of every day, and you'd open it up and you're like, "Man, that was for me, and, and that was for me, and God was speaking," and you'd go to church, and it'd be like, "God's speaking to me. It's like I'm the only one in the room. And you'd have these divine appointments with people, where you're like, "I think I was supposed to say that, and that really helped."

But slowly church, and the fellowship of believers slowly became less important to you, and you put down his word and you stopped

---

[14] Jim Berg. *God is More than Enough* (Greenville, SC: BJU Press/Journey-Forth, 2010).

reading it so much. And then you didn't pray as much, and then you didn't see as much of the God activities in your life, and then one day, "Like, how did I get so far from God?" It wasn't that you were running as much as you were drifting from him.

Notice the pattern: Jonah denies the presence of God. Jonah falls asleep. This is the pattern of sin. We turn off God's presence in our lives, and then we begin to drift spiritually. Examine your life. Where are you asleep? Where is your soul deadening? Awake!

We have all made decisions that have left us with scars that we will not erase until glory. We all have within us the temptation to flee to our own personal Tarshish. We must not try to take control of our own lives. God is in ultimate control of your life. How foolish it is to run from the loving God who wants his peace and joy to fill your life.

Don't be so worried about the ships that God is breaking. Stop trusting in worldly comfort or earthly security. Trust in the Lord and come back to him if you have been straying.

What kind of storms is God using to get your attention? What is the storm revealing to you? Are you trusting in earthly refuges? Have you realized how good God is to tear them down? How long will it take for you to have a change of heart? How is God using the storm to change the way you think about him and his mercy toward others? What has God asked you to do that you haven't done?

God Never Sleeps

God never sleeps. He never slumbers. He never nods off and accidently allows you to stumble. No. Everything God does is intentional. He wants you to be broken and molded into Christ's image.

Psalm 121:4 | Behold, he who keeps Israel will neither slumber nor sleep.

The Lord is your good shepherd and watchman. He always watches over us. He's always in hot pursuit of his people. He'll never leave us or forsake us. The Bible says something amazing of God's pursuit of the child of God.

Psalm 23:6 | Surely goodness and mercy [*hesed*] shall pursue me all the days of my life, and I will dwell in the house of the LORD forever.

I love the Hebrew word for mercy, *hesed*. It means God's unrelenting love. God chases us down and throws us overboard into a place of helplessness where we can finally know God's sufficient grace and enjoy his unrelenting love. We ought to be like the Shulamite farm girl in the Song of Solomon, who, now married to King Solomon, looks back at how she loved to run with the king through the fields of Jezreel near her home of Shulem.

Song of Solomon 1:4 | Draw me after you; let us run…. We will exult and rejoice in you; we will extol your love more than wine.

We ought to be calling to God, "Let us run together! Your love is better than the best wine!" God promises to do whatever it takes to soften his hardened child. He never, never sleeps. He did that for Jonah by sending a great storm. God will do whatever it takes to bring you back home, on your predestined path of having a heart like Jesus. You are being molded into his image. If God needs a storm to make that happen, he'll bring it. If God sent his own dear Son down to earth to die to retrieve you, don't you think he'll send as many storms as he has to in order to keep you holy?

Conclusion

Jonah's worst nightmare was exactly what he needed. I can remember praying for my sister to come to Christ. God answered by allowing her to become anorexic. She was divorced before she was 21. She was self-medicating and really on the verge of death. That's not the answer I wanted from the Lord. But she had to come to that nightmare scenario in her life to see how badly she needed Christ. She tried running for years, but finally God chased her down. Now her husband is the pastor of a Bible preaching church in Independence, Louisiana. She could run, but she couldn't outrun God. God loves you. He's going to chase you down. He's going to chase your loved ones down. No one can outrun the love of God!

2 | JONAH 1:4-17

OVERBOARD

They said to him, "What shall we do to you, that the sea may quiet down for us?" For the sea grew more and more tempestuous. He said to them, "Pick me up and hurl me into the sea; then the sea will quiet down for you, for I know it is because of me that this great tempest has come upon you."

JONAH 1:11

When I was a child, growing up in Louisiana, I had the amazing experience of going "tubing" on the Tickfaw River. What could be more fun than riding behind a boat on an innertube at about 15 mph (13 knots)? Imagine riding on an inflatable donut, being towed behind a speedboat. There must have been 20 tubes attached to each other. Various people chose this joyride: little children held by their mamas, teenagers goofing off, and lots and lots of preteens, like myself. I was a lanky, weak kid, but I was fearless when it came to adventure. My mom was on the shore of the river that day, hobnobbing with other mothers. She might have caught a glimpse of me as the boat launched forward. This was no lazy river ride. We were going way faster than I expected which to me meant more fun! But suddenly, my fun experience literally sunk. I went overboard into the river. Somehow, I was sucked underneath the web of innertubes, and this grand expedition became my grave. Humans still can't breathe underwater unassisted, so I was in trouble. I struggled to pull myself back up, but I was paralyzed by the force of the water, and my body was wedged in this death-trap. I remember thinking, "This is how I'm going to die." I miraculously found an opening a tube or two down from my original tube. I clung to the tubes on both sides, desperately pulled myself up, and was grateful to breathe that Louisiana air. I got my wind back. With all my might (which wasn't much), I maneuvered and jangled myself through the opening one lanky leg at a time. From that moment on I kept my legs firmly above the water and onto the tubes! Whew. I escaped an early funeral.

Down, Down, Down

In our text, Jonah has his own "overboard" experience. Jonah doesn't want to go to Nineveh, the capital of the ancient Assyrian empire, which is modern day Mosul, Iraq. He goes "down" to Joppa. He goes "down" three thousand miles away to Tarshish. In our text, he is thrown down into the depths of the sea. And then he goes further down when a "great fish" swallows him up. He's so close from going down into Sheol, the grave, and meeting his Master, but God is not done with Jonah. There is so much God wants to get done in Jonah.

The Main Character: Yahweh

In our story, we see the main character, and it's not who we might think. The prophecy of Jonah is not just about the big fish. It's not just about Jonah, the whale, and the deep blue sea. The main character in Jonah's story is God. Every single chapter—in fact, every single verse—speaks of the grandeur of God, the grace of God, the sovereignty of God, the beckoning of God, the discipline of God, and most of all, the compassion, and the mercy of God. Everywhere you look in this tiny piece of ancient historical literature, God is there. He's always there. He is right in the middle of every interruption. He's teaching his prophet (and all of us) how to have his heart. Don't you want the heart of God?

In the book of Jonah, everywhere that Jonah goes, God is following him, and God is busy demonstrating mercy and giving out grace. We first see sailors repenting and turning to the true God, and then the hardest, baddest people in the world. God is gracious and merciful!

Jonah's Reasons for Running

And then you have Jonah. Jonah hears the call of God, and then he runs the other way. Why? Jonah has his reasons.

First, Jonah's comfortable. Comfort can numb the heart to God. He's serving God for all the good things. He's comfortable. He's got the "success syndrome" that many of us in the West have. We confuse comfort and success with being right with God. But when God threatens his comfort, he runs the other way. When God strips us of our comfort, the idols of our heart are revealed.

Second, Jonah thinks he's better than the Assyrians. Self-righteousness numbs our hearts to God. Jonah's on the run because he hates the Assyrians, and he doesn't think they deserve God's grace. He's told to go to the capital of the Assyrian empire: Nineveh. These were the meanest, baddest people on earth, maybe in the history of the world. Do you not know that "God so loved the world, that he gave his only Son" (Jn 3:16)? Put your name in the blank. Now put someone you might think is almost unsavable in that blank. Jonah's success was great in Israel, and he wasn't about to give any thought to the nasty Ninevites. When God says, *I want you to have success with the Assyrians, go to their capital city*, Jonah says, *No way*.

Third, Jonah is popular in his country. Politics and popularity can numb our heart to God. For Jonah, earthly politics has replaced a heavenly mindset. He loved popularity with people more than peace with God.

There is a national hatred against the Assyrians, of which Nineveh is the capital. Jonah loves Israel. Granted, the Assyrians want to destroy Israel. He's been a popular, successful prophet in a prosperous, expanding political landscape in his homeland. Jonah's ministry has been all about Israel's expansion, and Assyria, with Nineveh as its capital, is all about the demise of Israel. The Assyrians sack Israel in 722 B.C., less than thirty years after the events of Jonah takes place.

Jonah's Excuses

Jonah was so comfortable preaching to his own people. He didn't want to go near those nasty, pagan, uncivilized Ninevites. Moses had his excuses when God called him, "I'm slow of speech!" (Exo 3–4:17). Adam said, "It's the woman's fault" (Gen 3:12). Jeremiah said, "I'm too young!" (Jer 1:4–8). Remember this: there are no excuses for the child of God. One man told Jesus, "I have married a wife, and therefore I cannot come" (Lk 14:20). Any excuse is a good excuse for the wandering child of God. If you as God's child don't surrender, God will chase you down. For Moses, he sent a burning bush. For Jonah, God interrupted Jonah's placid sea voyage with a ferocious storm.[15]

Jonah's not so much running away from Nineveh and the Assyrians, as much as he is running away from God. He doesn't want God's heart. Scholars say it might have taken a year to go all the way to Tarshish. It was a place where Jonah could go and hide. It's so far away with such a great cost to get there, that it's likely he would never return. He's set aside his prophet's mantle, but God won't let him run too far.

Jonah runs but God won't let him hide. We can try to run, but God will not let any of his children go. No one can pluck us out of his hand (Jn 10:28). The point of the story is that we can't run away from the ever-present God. Wherever you may be running, he is already there. Jonah is cornered by God in the middle of a storm, breaking up his ship. He has no choice but to ask to be thrown overboard. Why does Jonah (and all of us) have to "go overboard" at times?

> Key Thought: God sends storms to sanctify his children. Even though we try to outrun him, his purpose of making us like Christ is impossible to resist for the child of God.

GOD SHOWS US HIS POWER (1:4-6)

We've all been in storms. And then we've all been in *storms*! You know, the ones where the TV weather people are telling you to run and hide in your basement. The ones where the trash can lids blow off and rattle down the street into your neighbor's yard. The ones where 1:00 in the afternoon looks like the middle of the night—a storm can come fast and furious, and the same is true in our lives. Jonah was asleep to God's great power. Look at the storm God sent to Jonah to awaken him.

God's Incredible Power Hurled

Jonah had his getaway ship, but God stopped it with a fierce storm. The Lord always controls the weather for his own ends. He controls all the elements. It is not only in the miracles like the passage of the Red

---

[15] Duane A. Garrett, *Explore the Bible: Adult Commentary: Hosea, Amos, Jonah (Winter 2012–13): Revealing the Heart of God* (LifeWay Christian Resources, 2013), 124.

Sea and the storm on the Sea of Galilee that 'the winds and the waves obey him' (Exo 14:21–22; Mt 8:23–27). The storm that tossed Jonah's get-away ship was a 'storm of the Lord' (Jer 23:19–20).[16] Jonah can't outrun the presence of God since God is everywhere and controls all things. This was no chance storm. Some people are storm chasers. This was God's storm that was actually chasing Jonah.[17]

Jonah 1:4 | But the LORD hurled a great wind upon the sea, and there was a mighty tempest on the sea, so that the ship threatened to break up.

God deals with his runaway prophet by hurling a great, tumultuous wind on the Mediterranean Sea, and a violent storm arises, endangering everyone in the ship.[18] William Banks writes:

> When a person decides to run from the Lord, Satan always provides complete transportation facilities. But of course, God always knows how to wreck Satan's transportation. Praise God for that![19]

Modern meteorology has documented the destructive power rogue waves, tropical cyclones, microbursts, and other weather phenomena that pose unique threats to ships at sea. Jonah's ship cannot contend with God's storm. You see, the storm described in this first chapter of Jonah was different. This storm is personal. It is of divine origin. God is after Jonah. John Calvin comments:

> In this very personal storm, Jonah encounters the certain purpose of God, so that being overtaken on the sea, he acknowledged that he had been deceived when he thought that he could flee away from God's presence.[20]

God corners Jonah with a supernatural storm to rescue the prophet from himself. The Lord has a second motive as well: to demonstrate his power to the pagan sailors in Jonah's ship.

---

[16] Gordon J. Keddie, *Preacher on the Run: The Meaning of Jonah*, Welwyn Commentary Series (Darlington, England: Evangelical Press, 1986), 28.

[17] John Calvin and John Owen, *Commentaries on the Twelve Minor Prophets*, vol. 3 (Bellingham, WA: Logos Bible Software, 2010), 32.

[18] Rosa Ching Shao, *Jonah (Asia Bible Commentary Series)* (Langham Global Library, 2019), 21.

[19] William Banks, Jonah: *The Reluctant Prophet* (Chicago: Moody, 1966), 20.

[20] Calvin and Owen, *Minor Prophets*, 33.

God's Incredible Power Felt

This is no minor storm, but a divine tempest. These seasoned mariners are scared for their lives. The crew of the ship on which Jonah sailed was a pagan and international crew because each sailor called out to his own god for safety.[21]

The Mariners Prayed

Jonah 1:5a | Then the mariners were afraid, and each cried out to his god.

The mariners prayed. The sailors felt God's power and begin praying as they have never prayed before, calling on any god who can still the chaotic forces of the sea. They feel the power of God even though they don't know him yet. Jonah wasn't praying. He was sleeping. God called the Jews to be a blessing to all the nations of the earth (Gen. 12:1–3), but whenever the Jews were out of the will of God, they brought trouble instead of blessing.[22] Jonah is bringing great trouble to these sailors.

The Mariners Prepared

Jonah 1:5b | And they hurled the cargo that was in the ship into the sea to lighten it for them.

The sailors prepared to save the ship and thew everything overboard they could. Precious metals, horses and mules, ivory and expensive foreign rarities had already been tossed. Few things were deemed worth saving with their lives so perilously at stake.[23] The only line they appeared unwilling to cross, in terms of what they were inclined to abandon to the furious waters was Jonah. The pagan mariners have more compassion and care for Jonah than he does for them. He knows who brought this storm, but what's he doing?

---

[21] Duane A. Garrett, *Explore the Bible: Adult Commentary: Hosea, Amos, Jonah (Winter 2012–13): Revealing the Heart of God* (LifeWay Christian Resources, 2013), 124.

[22] Warren W. Wiersbe, *Be Amazed*, "Be" Commentary Series (Wheaton, IL: Victor Books, 1996), 73.

[23] James Limburg, *Jonah: A Commentary* (Louisville, KY: Westminster/Knox Press, 1993), 49.

God's Incredible Power Ignored

Where is Jonah? He's "fast asleep" in the inner part of the ship. The sea is no place to go for peace and quiet. But Jonah was numbing himself to God's call and his word. He had turned off and tuned out. His heart was hard enough to sleep through a storm that could take his life.

Jonah 1:5c | But Jonah had gone down into the inner part of the ship and had lain down and was fast asleep.

When they found Jonah, he was sleeping. How could the prophet Jonah be sound asleep in a great storm? You've got to be pretty tired to sleep in a situation like that. Depression was also probably a great motivator for unhealthy rest for the prophet. Sin can numb a person. There he was sound asleep in the hold of the ship. The boat may have been tossing, turning, splintering; but incredibly Jonah was not. He was unaffected. That's what sin will do to us. It numbs us. We can get to a point where we don't feel God around us, even though his power is surging.

God's Incredible Power Entreated

Jonah won't pray to the Lord, so the sailors ask him to entreat the Lord God. They have to wake Jonah up! The sailors are afraid, tossing their livelihood out of the ship, while Jonah slumbers on.

Jonah 1:6 | So the captain came and said to him, "What do you mean, you sleeper? Arise, call out to your god! Perhaps the god will give a thought to us, that we may not perish."

Jonah's getaway ship was about to be ripped to shreds by the waves of the Mediterranean Sea. As the wayward prophet slept below the deck, the sailors watched the waves of the placid sea rise and fall like a soft blue carpet, but suddenly, the sea came alive. Like a sleeping giant awakened, the waves grew to over twenty feet high. God was after his prophet. God is willing to do whatever it takes to keep his covenantal promises to his people: "You will be holy as I the LORD am holy" (Lev 20:26). God is using the sea to contend with Jonah, but Jonah is asleep!

The Pagans Awaken the Prophet

The sailors called out their pagan gods. I can imagine the captain making sure everyone is working and praying. And then he sees form of a man sleeping in the bowels of the boat. The man appeared almost dead. His body was half submerged in the water that sloshed around him.

"Who are you and why are you sleeping?" We can hear the captain screaming above the shrieking wind. The sailors are aghast that Jonah is sleeping. They are almost a mouthpiece for God when they say to him: "Awake sleeper!" (1:6). Jonah somehow seemed impervious to the storm. He was awakened out of a dead asleep! A lot of Christians need that wakeup call.

I can imagine the captain taking hold of Jonah, waking him up, and throwing questions at him. "What are you doing? How are you not praying, man? My men call out in fear to Dagon, to Baal, to Asherah, to whatever god or goddess they can think of, but you hold tight to the railing by your bed and utter not a single word to your god."[24] Jonah was utterly disoriented. Nothing made sense. The captain continued to scream at Jonah, "Can you pray? If you can do nothing else, pray! Ask your god to help us. Pray to your god. Maybe he will hear you. Maybe he will save us."

The Pagans Entreat the Prophet

Don't miss this: Jonah fled from the pagans, because he wanted the comfort of popularity and pride. Now, God's put him in a place where the pagans are begging him to pray to the Lord. He didn't not want to talk to pagans about God in the first place. He certainly didn't want to lead them to faith in the Lord. Now he finds himself talking about God to the exact sort of people he was fleeing.[25]

The sailors on board the vessel with Jonah were most likely Phoenicians, pagans who came from a polytheistic culture. They worshipped a plethora of gods, each of which governed a different aspect of nature and was easily offended. So when trouble arose, like this savage storm on the Mediterranean, these men never knew who had done what to anger a particular deity. That's why "every man cried to his god."[26]

How could Jonah become so hardened? He liked building his own little kingdom in Israel, and now he's called to build God's kingdom. He turns away from God and loses his anointing. He loses his zeal. He

---

[24] James A. Long, *Jonah: A Tale of Mercy* (Durham, NC: Torchflame Books / Light Messages, 2016), 29.

[25] Timothy Keller, *Rediscovering Jonah: The Secret to God's Mercy* (New York: Penguin Publishing Group, 2018), 32-33.

[26] Shirer, *Life Interrupted*, 81.

loses his love for the Lord. I believe I know where Jonah was. Depressed. Numb. *Bitter at the Lord.* He doesn't like the ministry anymore. That's what sin does to a person. But God is good at making a hard heart soft. He takes the heart of stone and makes it a heart of flesh.

God is in control of this storm, and he uses these pagan sailors to awake his sleepy prophet. Jonah can't outrun God. No matter where Jonah goes, God is going to use everyone and everything around him to bring him back to God. He'll use sailors. He'll use storms. And God will do the same for you if you are his child. God rides on the wind of the storm. God is riding on the storm in your life. He's guiding it. He's sovereign. God wants us to stop sleeping as Christians. He wants us to awaken to his great power.

GOD SHOWS US OUR BACKSLIDING (1:7-10)

What's going on? An investigation of sorts ensues. As we see throughout this book, the pagans have softer hearts than Jonah's hard, self-righteous heart. They tremble at God's storm, while Jonah has to be awakened by the pagan sailors!

Our Backsliding Investigated

God uses pagans to investigate Jonah's backsliding. He's sovereign! He can use all people and circumstances to carry out his will and reveal the state of his own children's heart. The sailors get together and devise a plan to find out who exactly is to blame for their sea voyage disaster.

Jonah 1:7 | And they said to one another, "Come, let us cast lots, that we may know on whose account this evil has come upon us." So they cast lots, and the lot fell on Jonah.

How sad is it that Jonah knows the power of the true and living God but is asleep to it. He's literally "fast asleep" while God is at work. The pagan sailors on the other hand, are out of their minds with fear. They are the ones praying while the prophet of Israel is sleeping on and on. The sailors are hurling cargo as God is hurling a great wind. Such evasive actions are ridiculous when you are dealing with the Lord. The Lord does not want their cargo; he wants the obedience of his prophet Jonah! They don't know this yet, so in fear of death, they keep hurling.

Finally, since Jonah's God is the creator God of land and sea, they decide to call on this God of the storm, and cast lots, and in a way ask

God to identify the guilty party. The lot fell on Jonah. You know the Bible says that God is even in control of the lot.

Proverbs 16:33 | The lot is cast into the lap, but its every decision is from the LORD.

Matthias was chosen by lot to be an apostle to replace Judas (Acts 1:12-26). Some Christians use the lot today to make certain choices. In the early 1960s, my kids' great grandfather, Ira Wenger was one of ten men qualified as deacon/preacher in the Mennonite church in Wayland, Iowa. They lined up the men. In a Bible there were ten lots. They needed three preachers, so they had three long lots and seven shorter lots (pieces of paper). Ira took one of the lots, and it was the longer one. He began a life as a lay preacher that would last for decades. I still have stacks of his sermon notes.

Lots in the time of Jonah were a bit different as they would have used something like modern day dice. The captain would have taken a pouch usually of sheep knuckles—commonly used as playing dice in the ancient world—and emptied them into his palm. Each one took a sheep bone from the pouch, bleached bright white. But one of them was a brownish color. The captain then went from man to man who reached in and pulled out one of the bones. Each man closed his hand around the unwelcomed prize until all the others had chosen his lot. The captain reached his strong, weathered hand in the pouch to remove the final piece of bone. The sailors and Jonah stared at their closed hands, and then one by one they shifted their gaze to the captain. With a simple gesture, the ship's captain opened his palm to reveal his lot. Each sailor followed his example. There was Jonah, open hand—he had drawn the indicting lot. He was the guilty one. He could hide no longer.

God can even use these lost sailors to get ahold of his prophet. God knows where you live if you know what I mean. That reminds me of this new DNA technology that is very effective in chasing down criminals or in locating parents from those who have been adopted. For years the police couldn't find this one notorious criminal in California, but DNA profiles from various ancestry websites helped identify the now 72-year-old subject. Authorities had collected the DNA evidence from the 1978 crime scene. And forty-five years later, they found him and put him in jail. God doesn't need DNA to track us down. He made DNA. He knows right where we are. We are foolish if we think we can outwit God.

There is Jonah, surrounded by sailors with lots in their hands. And Jonah is holding the indicting lot. He's the guilty party.

Our Backsliding Discovered

God was about to reveal himself through a confession Jonah is forced to make. The gig is up. He can't just hide and sleep. He's got to tell the truth about who he is. He's about to tell them that he is running from the one true and living God, the Almighty. Listen to this interesting confession. They corner him. "Who are you? Where are you from?" It's fascinating.

Jonah's Faith Discovered

Jonah 1:8-9 | Then they said to him, "Tell us on whose account this evil has come upon us. What is your occupation? And where do you come from? What is your country? And of what people are you?" **9** And he said to them, "I am a Hebrew, and I fear the LORD, the God of heaven, who made the sea and the dry land."

The God of the Red Sea crossing. Jonah knows the power of God. He's confesses to the sailors that he is "a Hebrew." That's a distinctive term known throughout the ancient world. People had heard of the Red Sea crossing, and so "Hebrew" meant "to cross or pass over."[27] Now the sailors are even more disturbed. *You serve the God of the Passover? Your God beat Pharoah's great armies?*

The God of the heaven and earth. Jonah fears Yahweh, the one true God over all, the God of the Red Sea crossing, he says. All the heathen served local deities, more like little weak men in the sky, but Yahweh is the Creator of the world, Lord of heaven and earth. Jonah clarifies that Yahweh is not just a local deity that people worship. He's not an idol. He's "the God of heaven, who made the sea and the dry land" (1:9). Now the sailors clearly infer that flight from *that* God is futile precisely because he is omnipresent, being bound neither to land nor to sea (unlike almost all other ancient Near Eastern deities.[28]

Jonah knows the God who can take the roughest seas and calm them in an instant with the words, "Peace! Be still!" (Mk 4:39). Yet he

---

[27] James Strong, *Enhanced Strong's Lexicon* (Woodside Bible Fellowship, 1995), *'Ibriy* (5680).

[28] Daniel C. Timmer, *A Gracious and Compassionate God: Mission, Salvation and Spirituality in the Book of Jonah*, ed. D. A. Carson, vol. 26, New Studies in Biblical Theology (England; Downers Grove, IL: Apollos; InterVarsity Press, 2011), 67.

is sleeping, hiding below the deck, having given up on God. Sometimes it takes a storm to bring us back to our confession: "I am one of the redeemed! God has passed over me! I fear the Lord, the God of heaven and earth, the sea and the dry land."

The Sailors' Fear Demonstrated

Jonah 1:10 | Then the men were exceedingly afraid and said to him, "What is this that you have done!" For the men knew that he was fleeing from the presence of the LORD, because he had told them.

Notice the sailors have more faith than Jonah. They had heard about the God of the Passover. He defeated Pharoah's army. You can't run from a God who is infinitely powerful and ever-present. "What have you done?" In other words, "Have you lost your mind?"

They had even asked him, "What's your occupation?" He just says, "I'm a Hebrew, and I know the living God." That's enough information for the pagan sailors to be terrified! How ironic that the lost mariners have more fear of the Lord than Jonah, God's prophet.

You've heard the proverb: "familiarity breeds contempt." Somehow Jonah had lost his awe of God. For him it was all words and wit, but no longer any wonder. He lost his fear of God. Even in the midst of the demonstration of God's great power on the sea, Jonah was hopelessly backslidden. The sailors are trembling before the living God, but Jonah is hardened.

GOD SHOWS US HIS SALVATION (1:11-17)

It has tradition among the Jews from the earliest times to read the book of Jonah on the Day of Atonement, Yom Kippur.

It's interesting that this whole episode turns to bring salvation both to the sailors, who tremble before the Lord and appear to commit their lives to him, and then for Jonah, who even though he is swallowed by a great fish, is sanctified through it. Let's find out what happens next.

The Sanctification of the Believer

The ship still threatened to break into pieces. The sailors' lives were still at stake. So with their hearts racing and their voices shaking, they yelled with fervor at Jonah over the noise of the tumultuous storm, "What should we do to you that the sea may become calm for us?" They are tools in God's hands to sanctify Jonah.

The Confession of Jonah

Jonah 1:11-12 | Then they [*the sailors*] said to him [*Jonah*], "What shall we do to you, that the sea may quiet down for us?" For the sea grew more and more tempestuous. ¹² He [*Jonah*] said to them, "Pick me up and hurl me into the sea; then the sea will quiet down for you, for I know it is because of me that this great tempest has come upon you."

"What shall we do with you Jonah?" plead the sailors. Jonah shouts: "Toss me to the sea. Only then will Yahweh bring peace." On the surface, this seems to be a softening of Jonah's heart, but it's more likely that Jonah's heart is still hard. He'd still like to be running or sleeping. God could have stopped the storm had his heart changed. Instead of Jonah's heart being soft, it seems to remain hard, while the pagan sailors in this scene have softer hearts than God's prophet. How sad!

The Compassion of the Sailors

Jonah 1:13 | Nevertheless, the men rowed hard to get back to dry land, but they could not, for the sea grew more and more tempestuous against them.

The sailors could not bear to throw a fellow human being overboard. They had far more respect for life than the prophet Jonah did. They tried to row the ship to shore, but the more they tried, the higher the waves became. I can hear the captain, "Our ship is battered but not sunk. She holds, men, she holds, and she will hold. To the oars! We'll make for shore. Perhaps, if we show this Creator God of land and seea that we mean to take his prophet back, he will show us mercy. Row, men, row! Put your backs in it. To the oars! To the oars!"

The Intercession of the Crew

Suddenly, an impromptu prayer meeting began, not by the prophet Jonah, but by the sailors.

Jonah 1:14 | Therefore they called out to the LORD, "O LORD, let us not perish for this man's life, and lay not on us innocent blood, for you, O LORD, have done as it pleased you."

As the sailors began to catch their breath, Jonah heard the strangest thing. He could not make out all of what they were saying, but interspersed among the foreign words, he caught the name "Yahweh." They were calling out to the Lord. These pagan men who from the storm's onset had prayed to their gods were now beseeching the Lord for his favor. They called on the Lord and were assured in their hearts of what they must do.

"Prophet," the captain said to Jonah, "we will do as you say and cast you overboard. May the Lord have mercy on us. I, for one, am convinced that this God of yours is Lord of both land and sea. May he have the same mercy on you that he has had on us."

Jonah must have been trembling. He knew his time had come. He could no longer run from God. He thought he would die with his wife and kids near him, but here he was, in a faraway place, forgotten, and about to be thrown overboard by the touch of the cold, wet, rough hands of these seafaring men.

I can hear the captain pray as he looks toward heaven: "Please, Lord, do not let us die for taking this man's life. Do not hold us accountable for killing an innocent man, for we, Lord, are obeying you. May your will be done."

The Calm of the Storm

They ceased Jonah. He didn't fight them.

Jonah 1:15 | So they picked up Jonah and hurled him into the sea, and the sea ceased from its raging.

The captain motioned for the sailors to take hold of Jonah under the arms while another took Jonah's feet. They lifted him up. Jonah closed his eyes, not wanting to see the pained look on the sailors' faces. Jonah felt himself swing backward and then forward, over the rail of the ship. He was suspended for only a moment in midair. Then he felt himself freefalling. They hurled him into the sea. Yet it was not that the prophet fell into the water but that the waves rose up to consume him.

As Jonah disappeared under the surface, the raging wind above immediately became a gentle breeze, and sea ceased its fury and slowed to a calm. The dark clouds that had kept them in perpetual night parted, and the sun beat down upon the faces of the sailors on board the battered ship.

The Sign of Jonah

What does this supposed "death" of Jonah mean? We find out it is a picture of the work of Jesus, and his death, according to our Lord in the New Testament.

Jonah 1:15 | So they picked up Jonah and hurled him into the sea, and the sea ceased from its raging.

Jesus is fond of this book Jonah which would be read in the Jewish tradition as part of the liturgy of the Day of Atonement. This is appropriate, since Jesus said that Jonah is a sign of Jesus death and resurrection. In the New Testament, Jesus says how Jonah is a picture of his death and resurrection.

In fact, Jesus himself compared the sea that Jonah was tossed into, to a grave—Jesus' own grave in fact. Jonah is a picture of Jesus in our text today. When Jesus would read Jonah, he saw himself and told others so. Listen to Jesus' teaching on Jonah in Matthew 12.

Matthew 12:40 | For just as Jonah was three days and three nights in the belly of the great fish, so will the Son of Man be three days and three nights in the heart of the earth.

Just as Jonah would be thrown overboard and into the belly of the fish to calm the storm of his own sin, Jesus would be thrown overboard into the abyss to suffer and die for our sin. How so? Here we see that Jonah is seen as a scapegoat, a sacrifice, and a savior.

Jonah, a Scapegoat

On the Day of Atonement, the high priest would take two goats and cast lots over them. One goat was singled out to die while the other was driven into the wilderness (Lev 16:8–10).[29] These scapegoats bore the sins of the community and atoned for those sins by death and banishment. Jonah is a sort of scapegoat too, but a very imperfect one: his journey into the darkness and his selection by lot to die came with sinful motives. The true scapegoat is Jesus, the Lamb of God who takes away our sin. He freely took the role of both goats—dying for sin and

---

[29] Janet Howe Gaines, *Forgiveness in a Wounded World: Jonah's Dilemma* (Atlanta: Society of Biblical Literature, 2003), 148.

bearing the separation from God that sin brings—to bring us back into the presence of the Father.[30]

Jonah, a Sacrifice

The ship's crew saw that they would incur guilt in the sacrifice as they threw Jonah overboard, and yet to their amazement they found salvation through the sacrifice. God's storm ended when Jonah was thrown overboard. As he was sacrificed, the ship's crew was saved. All of this shines a light on how the death of Christ is a demonstration of God's love for us. We crucified the Son of God—that's our guilt in the sacrifice. Yet, like Jonah, Jesus chose to lay down his life for us—that is our salvation through the sacrifice. There is, of course, this obvious and very great difference between Jonah and Jesus: Jonah was thrown into the sea on account of his own sins; Jesus was nailed to the cross on account of your sins and mine. Jesus had no sins of his own and therefore was uniquely in a position to offer himself as the sacrifice for our sins.

Bearing your sin and enduring your punishment, Christ was stretched out on a pole, suspended between heaven and earth and rejected by both. Christ went into the eye of the storm and offered himself as the sacrifice absorbing the judgment of God. He endured all that hell is on the cross, so that you would never know what hell is like.[31]

Jonah, a Savior

We will see later that Jonah will prophecy Jesus' resurrection by coming out of the sea, out of the fish, and onto the dry land. He will make his way to Nineveh and preach repentance, sparing these hell-deserving sinners, and granting them God's gracious covenant love and kindness. The people there will receive God's salvation. This is the sign of Jonah!

The Salvation of the Lost

Not only would Jonah be greatly benefited by this storm, but the lost sailors would come to know the true God even through the prophet's disobedience. It just goes to show you that salvation is not of

---

[30] Iain M. Duguid, *Jonah: Grace for Sinners and Saints* (New Growth Press, 2019), 19.

[31] Colin S. Smith, *Jonah: Navigating a God-centered Life* (Ross-shire, Scotland: Christian Focus Publications, 2012), Kindle edition.

any of his leaders. At best we are very imperfect tools. But salvation is of the Lord! Look at how God awakens the sailors to the fact that he is the one true and living God, and there is no other, as these pagan Phoenicians had wrongly thought.

> **Jonah 1:16** | Then the men feared the LORD exceedingly, and they offered a sacrifice to the LORD and made vows.

Look at the incredible response of the heathen sailors. They turn their hearts to Yahweh. Notice they are using God's covenant name!

It turns out Jonah's storm didn't just do him some good; it had a radically beneficial effect on others too. The thunderous rainstorm caused enough fear among the unbelieving to prepare them for a God encounter of their own. These formerly pagan sailors were now having a worship service, making vows and dedicating themselves to the Lord God, creator of heaven and earth. But what happens to Jonah? They throw him overboard.

The men on the ship's deck stared at each other, mouths open. The captain cocked his head and lifted an eye to the cloudless sky he had truly never expected to see again. He shifted his gaze to his battered crew and saw that even the hardest of them smiled at their good fortune. "A sacrifice to the Lord of heaven and earth, the God of Jonah," he said in a firm but reverent tone as the deck gently rocked beneath their feet. Perhaps they had saved one last animal, in case they had survived. In celebration of the Lord who had redeemed them, they had their first fellowship meal: a peace offering to the Lord. They slaughtered the animal, maybe a goat or a lamb. The sea was now calm. In great awe and fear and celebration, they gave profound thanks to the Lord who had mercy on them.

The Sovereignty of God

> **Jonah 1:17** | And the LORD appointed a great fish to swallow up Jonah. And Jonah was in the belly of the fish three days and three nights.

Jonah's body hit the water, and suddenly, he plunged downward. It must've felt like thousands of icy fingers were taking hold of his body and pulling him ever downward. He struggled but soon became all the more entangled in seaweed, and testifies, "weeds were wrapped about my head" (2:5). He thrashed about trying to free himself. He needed air. His lungs were burning. His mind was fading to black. "This is it."

Jonah's soul was about to be released to God. He would appear before him at any moment. *"This is the end,"* he must have thought. But something completely strange and unexpected happened. Jonah felt some creature swallowing him. His surroundings had suddenly changed. Jonah was contained on all sides by something soft, wet, smelly. He pushed against the confining space. It pressed tightly in on Jonah forcing the little oxygen left in his lungs through his mouth, and then he inhaled expecting his lungs to fill with water, yet somehow, he drew in air. Just when Jonah thought God was finished with him, it was actually just the beginning of a new chapter. Three days and three nights he would spend in the belly of the great fish. And it would be a prayer meeting like no other. God had rescued his prophet. In his sovereignty he sent the fish. In his love, he was sanctifying his prophet.

It was "the LORD" who appointed this fish to swallow up Jonah. If you've hit rock bottom, you know you are either going to cling to God and grow your faith, or you are going to check out and try to escape. We are called to grow from "one level of glory to the next." That took Jonah three days in the belly of the great fish. God knows how long we need at rock bottom to do his work. He knows best, and he wants your best and my best. Here is the comfort: if you belong to the Lord, you are in his good hands. The worst situation you are facing might turn out to draw you closer to God than ever before.

Conclusion

During the summer after my junior year of college, I worked as an iron worker at National Bullet Proof, near Chicago, Illinois. We made bullet resistant doors and windows made of steel. That steel came to us cold and hard and flat. We had to put it under an immense amount of pressure to bend it. At times we would use 20,000 pounds on a tool and die machine to crush that steel and form it into what we wanted it to be. We made bullet resistant doors and windows and wall panels.

God is making something far more precious. He crushes us and heats us up in the places he wants to bend us so that when he is done, we will be the exact form he wants us to be—the image of Christ. And we will be like those bullet resistant doors and windows. Even if the enemy comes at us, we are bulletproof from the fiery arrow of the enemy. His greatest schemes cannot defeat us, as long as we are in the master's care.

Yes, God's presses do hurt. There's pain and deep suffering in many of the trials you are going through. But let God form you in those moments. You may not like being in the belly of the fish, but God is humbling you so that he can use you. For Jonah it meant preaching to the Ninevites. For you, it is the expansion of God's kingdom in some way through evangelism or discipleship or both. But just know that fish has good purposes for you. That fish is going to get you where you need to be for God's kingdom purposes.

3 | JONAH 1:17-2:10
A FISH AND A PRAYER

And the Lord appointed a great fish to swallow up Jonah. And Jonah was in the belly of the fish three days and three nights.
JONAH 1:17

In 1972 Joan Baez was a popular singer and activist who was always working on a cause. During the Vietnam War, she traveled to the capital city of Hanoi with a peace delegation and was there during an American bombing campaign that lasted 12 days. She heard the explosions, saw the devastation, and was frightened to her core. She recalls that she learned to pray there.

> We spent the whole time in the basement of our hotel. I have never been so afraid in my life. I thought I was going to die. But I learned something—when the flames start coming towards you everyone starts praying, even the atheists and the agnostics, but when the flames start fading away, we all go back to the structures and beliefs that we had before.[32]

Even Joan Baez is no atheist in a warzone. We are going to see in Jonah how God is not impressed by the rote, mechanical and meaningless words that come from a cold heart. He has to take him to a place of complete vulnerability, like a warzone at the bottom of the sea. The

---

[32] David Watson, *Called & Committed* (Harold Shaw Publishers, Wheaton, IL; 1982), 83.

wants us to talk to him like a needy child. He tests us through hardships and trains us in humble supplication through difficulties. Jonah's prayer in the belly of the fish.

Before us is the story of how Jonah had to be stripped of comfort, all security, and all his prejudices, at least for this moment. With this deep stripping of his life, he was able to feel and know the presence of God like never before. This is Jonah's "undone" moment. Remember Isaiah's words.

Isaiah 6:5 | Woe is me! For I am lost; for I am a man of unclean lips, and I dwell in the midst of a people of unclean lips; for my eyes have seen the King, the Lord of hosts!

God's pursuit of you may come in the form of a great fish for Jonah, but for you it is a tragedy, a life-changing trauma, a betrayal, or a trial that won't go away. You are exhausted. But are you broken? Are you surrendered? God brings us to a point in our life to know him. Maybe you feel like God is being silent. Sometimes the people who suffer the most often feel God's silence the most. They feel abandoned.

Precious child of God, you may feel so blinded by your suffering, you may feel numb to God. Don't miss what God is doing. He's calling on you to trust in him. Lean not to your own understanding (Pro 3:5-6). He wants your full surrender.

God doesn't hide from us. We hide from God. C.S. Lewis in his book *Miracles*, reminds us that God never hides, but he is waiting for us to return to him. Lewis describes it as a game of cosmic hide and seek. We inwardly are hoping we don't find him. Suddenly, we sense someone or something breathing. He says God is not some impersonal silent object, but the living, breathing designer of everything about you:

"Look out!" we cry, "it's alive." ... Supposing we really found him? We never meant it to come to that! Worse still, supposing he had found us?[33]

You may be angry. You feel God is hiding. What if you do find God, or more correctly, he finds you? To know him, first you must be stripped of everything.

Jonah preached about God eloquently to the people of Israel, but his greatest encounter with God is in the belly of a fish. The fish that

[33] C.S. Lewis, *Miracles* (New York: Touchstone, 1996), 124–125.

strips Jonah of everything, even the hope of life itself, is actually a gift of grace from God.

A Fish Called Grace

In the life of Jonah, we find out that he's been thrown overboard by the Phoenician sailors. They've been converted and are worshipping and praying and offering sacrifices to the Lord of creation. Jonah surely thinks he is going to die in the sea. He is abandoned in the midst of the fierce and stormy Mediterranean Sea. And yet, he is not abandoned. God appoints a whale to swallow Jonah in order to save him from drowning. The great fish looks scary and strips Jonah of everything but is actually a vessel of God's grace!

> **Jonah 1:17** | And the Lord appointed a great fish to swallow up Jonah. And Jonah was in the belly of the fish three days and three nights.

The story of Jonah may sound outlandish at first, and we ask the important question: can a story like this be true? Is it even possible for a man to live inside a whale? On one hand, there shouldn't be much debate for the child of God since our God is the God of miracles. This event could have happened either way since God can suspend the laws of science to make his point to his prophet.

The Massive Size of Sea Creatures

Scientifically speaking, a human can survive in the belly of a fish, and it has actually happened in recent history. it is not impossible to survive in a whale. A sulphur-bottom whale and a whale shark have no teeth. They feed by submerging their lower jaw and straining out the water, swallowing any food. At one time, a one-hundred-foot Sulphur Bottom whale was captured off the coast of Cape Cod. The mouth was about twelve feet wide, big enough to swallow a horse. These kinds of whales have four to six compartments in their stomachs. A man could find lodging in any one of these compartments. In the head of this whale is a wonderful air storage chamber. It is an enlargement of the nasal sinus passage measuring seven feet high, seven feet wide, and fourteen feet long. If the whale has an unwelcome guest, giving him headaches, he swims to land and rids of his offenders.[34]

---

[34] Rod Mattoon, *Treasures from Jonah*, Treasures from Scripture Series (Springfield, IL: Rod Mattoon, 2003), 62–63.

Sailor James Barley

In February 1891, sailor James Barley and another sailor went missing as they capsized while harpooning sperm whales. The whale was found and put to death, and its blubber removed. The next day its stomach was hoisted onto the deck, and inside was sailor James Bartley, who was unconscious but shockingly alive. After being revived, he resumed his duties aboard his ship.[35] There is no debate as to whether this is possible since we have the first-hand account of this in recent history.

The Bleached Sailor

Ambrose John Wilson (in 1927) wrote about a case of a whaling ship sailor near the Falklands who was swallowed by a large sperm whale. Later the whale was harpooned and when it was cut open on deck, the surprised crew found their lost shipmate unconscious in its belly. Although the sailor had been bleached by the whale's gastric juices, the deathly looking whiteness never left his face, neck and hands.[36]

An Ancient Jonah Seal

Not only that, but we have also more than the biblical account recording Jonah's episode with the fish. There is a seal of the ring belonging to the reign of Amasis II of Egypt (570–526 B.C.) that shows with remarkable clarity a man emerging from a whale. The figure has been identified by the archeologist who discovered it as Jonah.[37]

Not About the Work Inside the Whale but Jonah

Now we don't want to spend so much time focusing on what happened inside this fish. Our text focuses on what happened inside Jonah! Jonah had turned and ran from the presence of the Lord, but the Lord would not turn from Jonah. Instead, he sent a fish after Jonah. Here

---

[35] Richard D. Phillips, *Jonah & Micah*, ed. Richard D. Phillips, Philip Graham Ryken, and Iain M. Duguid, Reformed Expository Commentary (Phillipsburg, NJ: P&R Publishing, 2010), 65.

[36] Ambrose John Wilson, "The Sign of the Prophet Jonah and its Modern Confirmations," *Princeton Theological Review, vol 25* (1927), 636.

[37] James Montgomery Boice, *The Minor Prophets: An Expositional Commentary* (Grand Rapids, MI: Baker Books, 2002), 284, *cf* Frank Knight, *Nile and the Jordan* (London: James Clarke & Co., Ltd., 1921).

we meet a fish called grace! God used this great difficulty to do good to Jonah and to the population of Nineveh. Our difficulties and trials in life are an expression of the grace of God because they make us stronger as believers.

Jonah is not praying at all in chapter 1. God puts him in a situation now where he has to pray. It happens to be in the belly of a great fish. God's gracious nature toward Jonah is intent on turning this stubborn man to a tender man. If you work your way through Jonah's prayer, you notice something happening inside Jonah. His heart is changing.

> Key Thought: Everything in the life, including the greatest pressures and the greatest delights are God's gracious chisels that conforms us into the image of Christ and bring us the highest joy that can be experienced in God alone.

THE GRACE OF DIFFICULTY (2:1-2)

Jonah was curved inward. Martin Luther once said that man is hopeless without Christ for a very clear reason.

> Man is "incurvatus in se" (Latin for "bent/curved inward toward oneself."[38]

He said this even before we had smartphones and tablets. It takes a great fish swallowing Jonah, but we finally see the prophet has stopped running, stopped sinking self and is praying to God. Jonah begins to pray. When he hits the water, he recognizes he is in serious trouble. He's stripped of everything, and this frees him to begin to pray. Jonah is in the middle of the Mediterranean, and he is at the express mercy of God.[39]

Maybe you find yourself there right now. You've been running from God, if you are honest. Suddenly life has gone dark. Let me ask you, what's your whale? What is it that is crushing you and bringing you to see your need of Christ? Realize that God is in charge of the great fish (and small fish) in your life. Embrace God's sovereignty and do as Jonah did: pray.

---

[38] Martin Luther in Mark Johnston, *Saving God: Religion After Idolatry.* Princeton, NJ: Princeton University Press, 2009), 88.

[39] Redmond, *Exalting Jesus in Jonah*, Jon 2:1–10.

Difficulty Leads Us to Supplication

Jonah 2:1 | Then Jonah prayed to the LORD his God from the belly of the
fish.

The place of prayer. There was Jonah in the belly of the fish. He
was no longer ignoring God's call. God gave him a foam blubber mat-
tress. Slimy. Dark. Gloomy. He had to be afraid. Surely, he was tempted
to despair. But instead of despair, difficulty sends Jonah to prayer, like
it does most of us. Jonah had been running from God, enjoying his
comfort zone. Difficulty is a wonderful tool from God to get Jonah back
on track. What is it that is revealing your deep weakness, your powerlessness, your total inability to change your circumstances? Don't get
bitter. This place of suffering is the blessing that brings you to God in
prayer.

The breakthrough of prayer. So much is happening inside Jonah
that wasn't possible when he was comfortable in his town near Nazareth. How long had it been since Jonah had opened his heart to God?
How long since he had prayed, really, from the depths of his soul? As
far as we can tell, praying is not something he had done since we first
met him exiting from Samaria near Nazareth on his way to Joppa.
Throughout the whole storm sequence of chapter 1, everybody is praying except Jonah. In chapter 2, every single word of Jonah's is a prayer.
Jonah knew God heard him before the answer came. This shows that
Jonah had faith and that God can give us a total peace and assurance
that our prayers are answered, even before the actual answer comes.[40]

Difficulty Leads Us to Surrender

God heard Jonah's prayer. In the prophet's distress, he had a confidence in God's mercy and compassion, that God had heard his prayer.

Jonah 2:2a | I called out to the LORD, out of my distress, and he an-
swered me.

It takes a near death experience for Jonah to surrender. He's tum-
bling down, down, down, to the bottom of the Mediterranean Sea. Tan-
gled in seaweed, light is dissipating, and darkness is growing. He's going to die, but suddenly, a fish called grace engulfs him.

[40] David Guzik, *Jonah*, David Guzik's Commentaries on the Bible (Santa Barbara, CA: David Guzik, 2000), Jon 2:1–2.

Not sure where he is, he feels the cavity of his new home. Slime and muscle are all around. He can hear the sound of a faint drum that has the rhythm of a heartbeat. He is able to breathe. How is he breathing under the sea?

"I'm alive!" he must've thought. Hope rises in a heart that was despairing. Though so close to death, Jonah suddenly feels more alive spiritually than perhaps ever in his life. In this grave of the fish's belly, it seems his faith has been renewed. As it is with God's true children, like a baby cries, the child of God prays. Jonah cannot help but to pray.

As Jonah prays, we hear what is already in his heart. We hear someone well acquainted with the Bible and with the Psalms in particular. Jonah is convinced that this fish is actually not a punishment, but a deliverance. He could have been swallowed up by the sea and dead on the bottom of the Mediterranean. But instead, we are introduced to a fish called grace. This awful place inside the fish is actually a salvation and deliverance for Jonah. With one foot already in the grave, he calls out to the Lord in surrender, and the Lord listens.

This wasn't just some "hail Mary" prayer. This was a true plea of surrender to the God of mercy and grace. We know that "God resists the proud but gives grace to the humble" (Jas 4:6). God doesn't listen to the proud, but only to those who come in childlike humility. Jonah was crushed. He surrendered in broken humility. And that's a good thing for every child of God.

Difficulty Leads Us to Singing

Jonah 2:2b | Out of the belly of Sheol I cried, and you heard my voice.

Jonah is peering into Sheol, to what he really deserves: the grave, and even worse, eternal punishment. We find out later he begins quoting the Psalms. He's likely singing the Psalms! Suddenly he realizes that this fish surrounding him is not a prison, but a salvation. God is with him, and this is God's way of teaching Jonah, as verse 9 says: that "salvation comes from the Lord."

For Jonah, this unusual salvation is something to sing about. It's clear that he's singing not only because of his constant reference to the Psalms, but also because his prayer is structured like the Hebrew hymnody in the Psalter. A study of Jonah's prayer will show allusions or references to Psalms 3, 5, 16, 18, 31, 40, 42, 50, 65, 73, 88, and 120.[41] The whole perspective of the psalms—on God and man, life and death, despair and hope, fear, and faith—is with God there is always hope. No matter where you are, God can bring beauty from ashes. He can redeem anyone from any hopeless circumstance.

As a prophet he is well acquainted with the Psalms, and as he is crushed inside the blubber of the whale, he prays and sings to God with a Psalm. What he is going to say is that this trial results in his salvation, a deliverance from the loving heart of the Lord. This fish crushes Jonah's self-dependance to pieces, and Jonah surrenders in an outburst of prayer with singing. Listen to his prayer.

Jonah 2:2 | I called out to the LORD, out of my distress, and he answered me; out of the belly of Sheol I cried, and you heard my voice.

This is the introduction to Jonah's Psalm or hymn. "I'm crushed, I'm calling, and God is answering." In other words, "God is with me. He heard my voice. He hasn't abandoned me." There is a confidence that God is with Jonah and that he hears him. Jonah not only understands the omnipresence of the Lord, he experiences it. "I'm in the belly of the fish, distressed, but God is with me, and he hears me." That's something to sing about.

Jonah's in the belly of the fish, and he is able to have something all the green pastures of Galilee couldn't give him. His heart and mind are now less consumed with his comfort on earth and now consumed with his destiny for eternity. Jonah says that he calls to God from the belly of "Sheol" which is a reference to the grave. He's saying he's as good as dead! And yet he is not abandoned there. God has not cut him off but graciously hears his cry. That's something to sing about.

Are you in a place of difficulty? One good exercise is to write a hymn or psalm of lament to God. Take Jonah's prayer and place yourself in it. Make it personal. Write it out to God. God will hear you. You may also want to make sure you have a good diet of Christian music. Secular music can be beautiful, but it is often very self-focuses and even depressing. Find some good worship music and give your burdens to the Lord. Sing! Pray! God hears you.

---

[41] Richard D. Phillips, *Jonah & Micah*, ed. Richard D. Phillips, Philip Graham Ryken, and Iain M. Duguid, Reformed Expository Commentary (Phillipsburg, NJ: P&R Publishing, 2010), 76.

THE GRACE OF DETACHMENT (2:3-7)

Jonah is cast into the deep. He's detached from normal life and completely alone. It's just him and the great fish, and fish don't like to make a great amount of conversation! We should be careful about solitude if it keeps us from the body of Christ, but often during times when God wants to bring great change to us, God will put you in a time of solitude with large segments of time when you are alone. God uses this time for you to get to know him. For Jonah, he was sinking to the bottom of the sea, and God sent a fish to remake Jonah into a tender, humble, attentive prophet.

God did this for me in November 2018 when a Ford F-350 hit my vehicle from behind and pushed me into oncoming traffic. I had a major concussion that required that I be alone in the dark most of the time to give my brain time to heal. It was a time of deep wrestling with God for me.

God's Providence in Our Solitude

God's presence meets us in our mess, wherever we are. He begins to quote Psalm 88:6. "You have put me in the depths of the pit, in the regions dark and deep."

Jonah 2:3a | For you cast me into the deep, into the heart of the seas, and the flood surrounded me.

God is sovereign over our mess. The fish that swallowed Jonah was not arbitrary but sent by God himself. The first thing Jonah says is, "You cast me in to the deep." God appointed the fish to swallow Jonah (1:17). Jonah realizes that it was not the sailors that cast him into the sea, it was God himself. Jonah sees that he has never been out of God's hands, though he tried to run from him.

When we think of God's promise to sanctify us, it means that God will go to whatever lengths are necessary to do it. He who began the work in you is committed to completing it in you (Phil 1:6). We are predestined to be conformed to Christ's likeness (Rom 8:29). Whatever it takes! That means, first, that God meets us in our mess.

That is why he comes to the young prodigal in the pigsty, and he meets him there (Lk 15:11–24). That is why he comes to Jonah in the stomach of the fish, and he meets him there. Both are in stinking situations, literally. The prodigal is surrounded by pigs, and Jonah is engulfed in the very gut of this large fish. And both in the pigsty and in the fish's stomach, God was coming to meet them, to clean them up, and to restore them to his glorious purposes.

God's Word in Our Solitude

God's word steadies us in our solitude. Don't miss this. Jonah begins to quote the Psalms. Sometimes we are laid up and don't even have access to a Bible, but we've treasured God's word in our heart. As the waves washed over Jonah, so the word also washed over him.

Jonah 2:3b | All your waves and your billows passed over me.

As Jonah realizes God's presence, he throws himself on the foundation of God's word as he quotes Psalm 42:7, "All your waves and your billows passed over me" (*cf* 2:3a). He knows other saints have been where he is. When we are in a mess, God's Spirit reminds us of the treasure of God's word we have stored up.

It's ironic that Jonah's prayer shows that he is well-acquainted with the beautiful truths from the psalms, yet he appears not to have grasped their applications.[42] Like so many of us as believers, it is far easier to memorize the Bible and its truths than to live them out. It's usually in our mess that we begin to really hold strongly to the word of God and see its steadying effect on our lives.

God's word is the only meaningful cure for sin. God's word alone can transform you into the image of Christ, from one level of glory to another (2 Cor 3:18). Psychology cannot help us. At times psychology can indicate something is wrong, but so superficially. Listen to the words of Dietrich Bonhoeffer.

The most experienced psychologist or observer of human nature knows infinitely less of the human heart than the simplest Christian who lives beneath the Cross of Jesus. The greatest psychological insight, ability, and experience cannot grasp this one thing: what sin is. Worldly wisdom knows what distress and weakness and failure are, but it does not know the godlessness of man. And so, it also does not know that man is destroyed only by his sin and can be healed only by

---

[42] Kevin J. Youngblood, *Jonah*, ed. Daniel I. Block, Zondervan Exegetical Commentary on the Old Testament (Grand Rapids, MI: Zondervan, 2015), 105.

forgiveness. Only the Christian knows this. In the presence of a psychiatrist, I can only be a sick man; in the presence of a Christian brother I can dare to be a forgiven, growing sinner.[43]

The word of God alone is sufficient to not only get you loving God but hating sin because you "taste and see" and experience that God alone is good. God alone is like a filet mignon steak compared to the roadkill of sin. When Jonah is stripped of everything, he's able to see and savor the Lord through his word.

God's Faithfulness in Our Solitude

God's faithful reputation calms us in our mess. If you could hear Jonah in chapter 2, you would hear melody and rhyme and rhythm. This is a glorious poem, packed solid with God's word in the Psalms with promises of God's faithfulness.

> Jonah 2:4 | Then I said, 'I am driven away from your sight; yet I shall again look upon your holy temple.'

Jonah's prayer is filled with Scripture, this time quoting Psalm 31:22, "I am cut off from your sight." There is a place in the Christian life when we feel "driven away from God's presence." We sinned again. A tragedy or trauma has happened. A child has gone astray. A part of your life is cut off. A relationship is in turmoil. You are suffering. This is where we need to have hope that God will show up. God is faithful. Yes, hear it again. God is faithful! He began a good work in you, and he will complete it (Phil 1:6).

Jonah knows God's faithfulness through his word. We cannot get hope outside of the word of God. It is through God's word, his exceeding great and glorious promises!

> 2 Peter 1:4 | He has granted to us his precious and precious and very great promises, so that through them you may become partakers of the divine nature, having escaped from the corruption that is in the world because of sinful desire.

Change does not occur apart from resting in the faithfulness of God through is word. He feels "driven away from God's sight," yet he has hope that comes from God himself.

---

[43] Dietrich Bonhoeffer, *Life Together* (Dietrich Bonhoeffer Works) (Minneapolis, MN: Fortress Press, 2015), 95.

Jonah's greatest fear, to be driven away and exiled from God's nurture and care, is met with faith. Though he is in the belly of the great fish, and it feels like he is truly "cut off" from God's sight and care, yet, he has faith that he shall yet look again upon God in his temple.

Joni Eareckson Tada said, "God permits what he hates to bring to pass what he loves."[44]

God hates the paralysis of your child or of you. He hates that divorce you had to endure. There is the diagnosis of a birth disorder, or the distinct loss of a burn victim, or a life given for decades to addiction or immorality. Dreams are shattered for us, our children, our future. God's heart is broken over these things. Yet God permits these sufferings and sins so that people, in their weakness, in their suffering, and yes, in their sin can find the hope of Christ! God is in the redeeming business. God's power is displayed in our weakness (*cf* 2 Cor 4:7).

God can make it where there is a distinct beauty that would not happen without that brokenness. Some of you have a distinct glory over your life because God, in your life, brought beauty out of ashes. We think those ashes are unredeemable. God wants to bring beauty from ashes.

When our feelings tell us one thing (we are cut off from God), Jonah teaches us that we must preach to ourselves. He had a sure expectation that he would see the Lord's glory at his temple in Jerusalem. He refers to Psalm 73:17 about his hope of seeing God again in his sanctuary, his holy temple. He chose not to "lean to his own understanding" but to acknowledge the Lord through the hope of his word (Pro 3:5-6). God promises that neither our sin nor our circumstances will ever cut us off from his grace. Indeed, nothing can "separate us from the love of God in Christ Jesus our Lord" (Rom 8:39). God's faithfulness is something that can calm us as we realize he commands our steps and our destiny.

God's Mercy in Our Solitude

Jonah's choices were disastrous. He describes how he was headed straight for death. The bars of death were closing in on him. The fish does not show up as soon as Jonah hits the water. In cartoon versions

---

[44] Joni Eareckson Tada, "God Permits What He Hates," *International Disability Center* (Joni and Friends, January 31, 2014), http://registration.joni-andfriends.org/radio/4-minute/god-permits-what-he-hates2/.

of this scene a huge fish opens its mouth and Jonah jumps right in with an Olympic diver's precision. That is not true to what happens here. Instead, Jonah hits the water, and the Lord allows him to sink awhile so that he might grasp the seriousness of the consequences of his choices.[45] Listen to Jonah's recollection.

> **Jonah 2:5-6** | The waters closed in over me to take my life; the deep surrounded me; weeds were wrapped about my head [6] at the roots of the mountains. I went down to the land whose bars closed upon me forever, yet you brought up my life from the pit, O LORD my God.

The *waters* close in on Jonah. He remembers how he hit the water and headed straight for death. It is the mercy of God that pretty much resurrects him. Before the fish swallowed Jonah, the Lord allowed him to sink awhile so that he might grasp the seriousness of the consequences of his choices.[46] Has the Lord allowed you to sink? Are you grasping his mercy in this time? The descent and humiliation of the child of god are never a result God's wrath, but his mercy. He's the surgeon cutting out the cancer. He's the trainer putting the weights on you to make you stronger. He's the eagle pushing you out of the nest and into the air so you can fly.

The *weeds* close in on Jonah and wrap around his head. Look at Jonah's horrifying description of his descent to the bottom of the Mediterranean. He personifies the waters like a wrestler who was strangling the life out of him. The seaweed has him in a headlock (2:5). Surrounded on every side, Jonah is a prisoner of the sea.[47]

The *grave* closes in on Jonah. Jonah goes as deep as you can go, "to the roots of the mountains" (2:6a) to the bottom of the Mediterranean Sea. Jonah looks at the bottom of the sea as a prison "whose bars closed upon [him] forever" (2:6b). Death has him and will not let him go. But then something wonderful happens. Jonah testifies that even in his most desperate time, God in grace was pursuing him.

---

[45] Eric Redmond, William Curtis, and Ken Fentress, *Exalting Jesus in Jonah, Micah, Nahum, Habakkuk* (Nashville, TN: Holman Reference, 2016), 30.

[46] Ibid.

[47] Donald J. Wiseman, T. Desmond Alexander, and Bruce K. Waltke, *Obadiah, Jonah and Micah: An Introduction and Commentary*, vol. 26, Tyndale Old Testament Commentaries (Downers Grove, IL: InterVarsity Press, 1988), 127.

The *grace* of God closes in on Jonah. God in mercy pursues him (Psa 23:6). Listen to Jonah's testimony, "Yet you brought up my life from the pit, O LORD my God" (2:6c). The fish acted as Jonah's rescue boat! He's again singing—this time Psalm 40.

> *Psalm 40:2* | He brought me up also out of an horrible pit, out of the miry clay, and set my feet upon a rock.

Though he is in the slimy belly of the whale, Jonah praises God that he is not dead, but that he's very much alive. The fish rescued him from being buried at the bottom of the Mediterranean Sea. Jonah, in a sense, was brought back to life from the pit. It reminds me of what Paul says in Ephesians.

> *Ephesians 2:4-5* | God, being rich in mercy, because of the great love with which he loved us, ⁵even when we were dead in our trespasses, made us alive together with Christ—by grace you have been saved.

In salvation, God makes us alive when he regenerates us by the Holy Spirit. He also does this throughout our walk of sanctification. Whenever we stray from the Lord, we die a death, and God brings us to repentance and to experience the Holy Spirit's resurrection power anew and afresh. No Christian can live comfortably in a life dominated by sin. "Sin will have no dominion over you" (Rom 6:14a). God will send his great fish for his children as they are sinking down. God brings his children closer during their times of suffering and trial. He recovers his children from a life of sin and selfishness. He draws us near, even if the trials and suffering are painful.

God's Presence in Our Solitude

> **Jonah 2:7** | When my life was fainting away, I remembered the LORD, and my prayer came to you, into your holy temple.

How ironic that Jonah is able to sense the overwhelming presence of God, not in Israel, not with his people, not in his ministry, but on the bottom of the floor of the Mediterranean Sea. Remember this is Jonah praying before the fish came. In response to Jonah's prayer, God sends the fish! Be careful how you pray. Deliverance for us is often the belly of a fish. Are you ready to pray like Jonah? "Lord, deliver me whatever it takes." That's a wonderful way to pray. God will deliver you. It is in this darkest, most detached of places that Jonah communes with God. He has no strength, and God's power rests upon him in his weakness (2 Cor 12:9).

Jonah was all alone at the bottom of the sea, and that became his prayer closet. That place where we are utterly broken and alone before God is a holy, sacred place. When we come to the end of ourselves, and we are utterly powerless, that's the time we learn to pray. God's power reinvigorates our prayer life. The school of prayer is taught to us when we are in the place of greatest peril. It is then we truly grasp our own powerlessness and the absolute need for God's power. That's how we are to live the Christian life, constantly dependent on God's power. This is what Jesus told Paul when he was so weak.

2 Corinthians 12:9 | My grace is sufficient for you, for my power is made perfect in weakness.

How weak Jonah felt as his "life was fainting away." As a prophet and believer in the Lord, he merely needed to remember the Lord the glory and greatness of his God, which he did, and God answered his prayer... with a great fish. Gulp! There goes Jonah!

THE GRACE OF DELIVERANCE (2:8-10)

The fish seemed more like a coffin of incarceration than a vehicle for deliverance. Jonah testifies that the confinement of the fish brought freedom, because this near-death experience woke him up spiritually and rescued him from himself and all his idols.

Delivered from Idols

Jonah 2:8a | Those who pay regard to vain idols forsake their hope of steadfast love.

Now Jonah quotes Psalm 31:6, "I hate those who pay regard to worthless idols." It wasn't just the Ninevites and the pagan sailors that were idol worshippers. Those amongst his own people in Israel were known to cling to these worthless idols. They worshipped the Baals. He had to preach against his own people with fellow prophets. Jonah came right after the ministries of Elijah and Elisha. He preaches alongside Amos and Hosea. Isaiah comes just after Jonah.

The Personal Nature of Idols. It wasn't just the sailors, and the wayward Israelites that had idols. Many idols had snuck into Jonah's heart. We all have idols. The word translated 'idols' means literally a snare or a trap.[48] Idolatry is a worship issue when our heart longs for comfort or pleasure or power or possessions or worldly peace more than God. Tim Keller's definition of an idol is helpful.

> An idol is whatever you look at and say, in your heart of hearts, "If I have that, then I'll feel my life has meaning, then I'll know I have value, then I'll feel significant and secure."[49]

Idols are identified when we don't get what we want. Take this illustration from Robert Jones[50] for example. Jesus alone must have the throne. Idols vie for position in our hearts to displace God. It could be a really good thing. You start out well. Desiring to please God in your marriage, but now you're trying to control your marriage. You love ministry, but ministry can displace God in your heart. You try to have a godly marriage, but now you want people to love you, and you are angry if your reputation is sullied because of marriage struggles. Anything can become an idol.

JESUS ALONE MUST HAVE THE THRONE

A B C D E F G

---

[48] Donald J. Wiseman, T. Desmond Alexander, and Bruce K. Waltke, *Obadiah, Jonah and Micah: An Introduction and Commentary*, vol. 26, Tyndale Old Testament Commentaries (Downers Grove, IL: InterVarsity Press, 1988), 129.

[49] Timothy Keller, *Counterfeit Gods: The Empty Promises of Money, Sex, and Power, and the Only Hope That Matters* (Riverhead Books, 2011), xviii.

[50] Robert D. Jones. *Pursuing Peace* (Wheaton: Crossway, 2012), 65.

The throne with cross represents the Lordship of Jesus Christ in our lives. We must keep Jesus first!

We cannot serve two masters. So when something takes the place of Jesus' throne and kicks the Lord off the throne, we start to protect that idol in our life. We love it, and we get anxious or angry or despairing if the idol is threatened. We don't want to lose it. It could be your finances. It could be a life-dominating sin. It could be a good thing or a bad thing, but it's taken the place of Christ. Get rid of any staircases that lead you to trust and rest in idols. Keep the good gifts of God under the lordship of Christ. Don't love sin and cherish it. We as Christians see sin as roadkill. It should turn our stomach.

Can I get a witness that it's better to go hungry than to eat roadkill. Therefore, we need to get used to living with unmet desires in this life. Don't feed the flesh. Real satisfaction comes from submitting all our desires to Jesus.

> A large part of the art of living for Jesus is learning to live contentedly with ongoing unmet desires. When my desires remain submitted to Christ, my soul finds rest. Inner peace reigns. —Robert Jones, Southern Seminary, "Pursuing Peace"[51]

The Powerful Nature of Idols. Jonah's idolatry of himself, of his politics, of his own comfort zone is radical and powerful. Idolatry cannot be played with. It's life dominating. It had launched his heart and

---

[51] Ibid.

his feet in the wrong direction. He had to forsake his idols before directed rightly again. We are going to see that even when Jonah gets back to doing God's will, he relapses in chapter 4. But it seems he writes this book as a testimony to his own waywardness, and God's grace to rescue his wayward children.

The Powerless Nature of Idols. Idols promise superhuman results. They are false saviors, but they cannot deliver. Jonah calls them "vain idols" which in Hebrew is literally *"empty nothings."* Idolatry is dangerous for many reasons, one of the most prominent being that idols cannot save and will never satisfy.[52] You need peace? Throw back some alcohol. Look at some porn. Microwave your pleasure. You need security? Be manipulative and controlling. Lie to get more money from your employer. Steal. That's the lying nature of idols. Instead of trusting in God's *hesed*, his unrelenting love, Jonah had been trusting in his own way of thinking. Jonah says that clinging to idols is the way we forfeit the lasting hope and comfort of God's unrelenting love. We try to turn the gifts God gave to comfort us into our own personal messiahs. It may be the idol of *power* – we want to control the situations in life. We'll even use ministry or church to gain prominence and place and power. We live for *popularity* – we please people and let others control us. We allow the sin of co-dependence on *people*. We desire *prominence* and acceptance from humans instead of God. Listen, the only person we cannot live without is Jesus Christ. The idol may be *pleasure* – what do you flee to when you are hurting? That's your messiah. That's your Christ and king. That's your savior. The idol may be *possessions* and material things. Listen cars, homes and gizmos will not fill your cavernous heart. All things get their life and breath and being from God. How can those other things be sufficient saviors?

What's your identity and purpose in life? Is it your job, your family, your hobby, your bank account, your escapism, or is it "to glorify God and love him"? Jonah's fish was a gift of grace! The grace of deliverance came when that fish rescued him from himself and all his idols.

---

[52] Douglas Stuart, "Jonah," in *New Bible Commentary: 21st Century Edition*, ed. D. A. Carson et al., 4th ed. (Leicester, England; Downers Grove, IL: Inter-Varsity Press, 1994), 819.

Delivered for Steadfast Love

Jonah 2:8b | Those who pay regard to vain idols forsake their hope of steadfast love.

Jonah comes to a great realization in the belly of the fish: all the earth who worships idols are forsaking real hope and joy and peace through God's steadfast, covenant love. Real contentment is found in God's steadfast love alone. Try to find it anywhere else, and you are asking for major misery. You've got to put your trust in that which cannot be taken away. When we choose idols, we forsake the only thing that can satisfy the human heart (*cf* on Hos 6:4–6; Eccl 3:11).[53]

Delivered for Sacrifice

Jonah, now delivered from the jaws of death wells up with gratitude and worship to God. He wants to sacrifice. He wants to give everything he has to the Lord. His words echo the response of the sailors in 1:16.[54]

Jonah 2:9a | But I with the voice of thanksgiving will sacrifice to you; what I have vowed I will pay.

When all was stripped away, he saw the worthlessness of idols and the wonder of God's presence. Jonah was so overwhelmed he wanted to sacrifice. Being in the belly of a fish he had no ability to give a bull or a lamb to sacrifice to God, so he gave something much more precious to God, a sacrifice of thanksgiving.

After his sacrifice of praise, he gave all that he had: a vow of service to the Lord. He submitted and surrendered to the will of God. His vow meant that he would no longer be on the run. He would go to Nineveh and give the message God had for the Ninevites.

Delivered through Salvation

The great theme of the book of Jonah is expressed in five simple words.

---

[53] James Limburg, *Hosea–Micah*, Interpretation, a Bible Commentary for Teaching and Preaching (Atlanta, GA: John Knox Press, 1988), 149.

[54] Donald J. Wiseman, T. Desmond Alexander, and Bruce K. Waltke, *Obadiah, Jonah and Micah: An Introduction and Commentary*, vol. 26, Tyndale Old Testament Commentaries (Downers Grove, IL: InterVarsity Press, 1988), 129.

Jonah 2:9b | Salvation belongs to the LORD!

What was the renewed prophet's conclusion? "Salvation belongs to the Lord." The word for deliverance or salvation is *yeshua*. When the angel announced to Mary that she would have a son, he said, "you shall call his name Jesus [Hebrew, *yeshua*], for he will save his people from their sins" (Mt 1:21).[55] Jesus is our salvation!

From beginning to end, our salvation is completely in the hands of the Lord God. We deserve God's wrath. Without the Lord's mercy, we would all be destined for an eternity without Christ. But praise him with highest praise: salvation belongs to the Lord. Jesus bled and died for our sins. He rose again. He calls, he justifies, he sanctifies, and he glorifies. He is the Lord of salvation. It belongs to him, from beginning to end. We didn't invent it. We weren't looking for God. Salvation is not of us, not of works, not based in our ability to follow God. No, He chose us. He justifies. He grants us salvation from beginning to end. Salvation belongs to the Lord! The great prince of preachers, Charles Spurgeon said it this way.

> The plan of salvation is entirely of God. No human intellect and no created intelligence assisted God in the planning of salvation; he designed the way, even as he himself carried it out. No one instructed him. He himself alone, did it... Without God it could not have been devised. It is a plan too splendid to have been the product of any human mind... On yonder cross I see the man who "trod the winepress alone;" ... I see the solitary conqueror, who came to the fight single-handed, whose own arm brought salvation, and whose omnipotence sustained him. ... The Lord has to apply it, to make the unwilling willing, to make the ungodly godly, and bring the vile rebel to the feet of Jesus, or else salvation will never be accomplished.[56]

Salvation, indeed, belongs to the Lord, from beginning to end. He chose us before the foundation of the world. He justifies us by grace alone through faith alone in Christ alone. He did it alone! And he will sanctify us and glorify us! And he alone gets all the glory forever and ever and ever! Amen!

---

[55] James Limburg, *Hosea–Micah*, Interpretation, a Bible Commentary for Teaching and Preaching (Atlanta, GA: John Knox Press, 1988), 148.

[56] Charles Haddon Spurgeon. "Salvation is of the Lord" *The New Park Street Pulpit*, preached May 10, 1857 (London: Passemore and Alabaster, 1857), 193.

Delivered to Nineveh

Jonah 2:10 | And the LORD spoke to the fish, and it vomited Jonah out upon the dry land.

Jonah didn't know it, but as he was in the fish for three days and three nights, that fish was traveling. He was going somewhere. The text doesn't say, but it must have been in the direction of Nineveh. Wherever it was, Jonah was no longer in the belly of the fish. That sea creature "vomited Jonah out upon the dry land." From that dry land, Jonah obeyed the call of God and headed to Nineveh, the capital of the dreaded Assyrians.

Nineveh is 550 miles inland from the coast of Joppa, perhaps where the fish spit out Jonah. There was still a great distance between his starting point and his destination. But Jonah obeyed God. He was delivered by God from the fish's belly to go on a mission.

When our Lord came to the earth, he used the prophet Jonah's deliverance from the fish as an illustration of the gospel. That's where we need to be. Our focus should not be on Jonah or Nineveh, but on the Greater Jonah, Jesus Christ.

Matthew 12:40-41 | For just as Jonah was three days and three nights in the belly of the great fish, so will the Son of Man be three days and three nights in the heart of the earth. [41] The men of Nineveh will rise up at the judgment with this generation and condemn it, for they repented at the preaching of Jonah, and behold, something greater than Jonah is here.

There is, we see, a greater Jonah. And this greater Jonah suffered not because he was running from God, but he was a substitute for all those who run from God. Just as God appointed a fish for Jonah, he appointed Christ to be crucified according to his divine plan and purpose (*cf* Acts 2:23).

There is a greater Jonah! Our Lord "descended to the lowest parts of the earth" and conquered death and hell. Like Jonah in the fish, the grave released our Lord. It could not hold him! We have that same resurrection power. Walk in the resurrection power our greater Jonah, the Lord Jesus Christ.

Conclusion

Jonah drew near to God in the great fish. Look through your life, and you'll find the hard times were the times God drew you even nearer. When Jonah's deep in the belly of the fish, instead of powering his prayer life down, he powers it up. When we are in trial and tribulation, saints, we need to, more than ever, power up. But we'll see in the life of Jonah later, that he relapses into his idols. He starts arguing with God. He's so angry he wants to die. He was no longer in the belly of the fish, and he gets comfortable again. The comfort zone is a problem for every Christian. In the worst and best times, we need to power up our prayer lives.

During the 1980s there was a real problem with airplanes crashing on landing at the end of runways. During a thunderstorm, an updraft of wind would shoot out of the sky and push the plane up off the ground as it was trying to land. The pilot tried to throttle the plane down into the gust but would often end up crashing and destabilizing the plane. The engineer who studied it suggested that instead of throttling the plane down into the updraft, they should use the wind and throttle the plane up and through the updraft. This practice stabilized the planes, and the runway crashes ceased.[57]

It teaches us that when the easier times of life come, and we have an updraft, we ought not throttle down, but throttle up. It's easy to remember to throttle up in the hard times. But we need to throttle up and keep close to God in the updraft times, when things start getting easier, we need to power up our walk with God and draw close to him!

---

[57] Brian Chappell, "How to Illustrate", *Christ-Centered Preaching: Preparation & Delivery of Sermons*, (Covenant Theological Seminary, St. Louis, MO, Fall 2006), Lecture 14A, https://media.thegospelcoalition.org/wp-content/uploads/2017/11/10180057/CCP_T_Lecture_14A.pdf.

4 | JONAH 3:1-10
OVERTHROWING NINEVAH

The people of Nineveh believed God. They called for a fast and put on sackcloth, from the greatest of them to the least of them.
JONAH 3:5

I love to see something transformed. Our church's parsonage was once a gang house for the Latin Kings. I remember the gang signs throughout along with the vandalism. No one wants a gang house in their neighborhood. People in the town were mortified and afraid. With the help of some volunteer union laborers from Leopardo Construction, we gutted that place to its bare bones, put on a new roof, new siding, new windows. The community gathered for opening day with the mayor when we transformed that gang house into a Spanish community center, and then a parsonage.

In the text before us, we find the meanest, baddest city in the ancient world experience a revival of divine proportions. We see how powerful God's mercy is, and how the cruelest people can be transformed into a new creation. Their repentance was so radical, that Jesus used them as an example of repentance in the New Testament (*cf* Mt 12:39-41).

What is Revival?

When we speak of "revival" we are talking about the life of God in the soul of man. The dictionary says:

Revival is an awakening of people to their spiritual concerns.[58] —*Webster's Dictionary 1828*

I like what Leonard Ravenhill said about revival.

Revival is when God gets so sick and tired of being misrepresented that he shows up himself.[59] —*Leonard Ravenhill*

Lloyd Jones said that revival is something utterly supernatural.

A revival is a miracle. It is the hand of the Lord, and it is mighty. It can only be explained as the direct action and intervention of God. It was God alone who could divide the Red Sea.... Revival is a mighty act of God.[60] —*Martyn Lloyd-Jones*

Iain Murray gets to the heart of what revival is.

Revival is a manifestation of the presence and power of the Holy Spirit in an uncommon measure, bringing refreshment to the church and salvation to the world. But although it is a sovereign work of God, it is also a work performed in answer to petitions offered by a praying people.[61] — *Iain H. Murray*

In revival, God moves in what we think is an unusual way, where people are brought closer and deeper in their relationship with him. Often, in revival, there are great numbers of conversions as well. This is what Nineveh experienced.

It is my conviction that God wants to give all his people revival. We simply need to seek him in prayer for personal revival, as Jonah did, and God will pour out his grace through us. He may even overthrow the devil's power over your city as he did in Nineveh.

How does one man, without military or political power – without power over the learning institutions or philosophical empowerment walk into one of the greatest cities in the ancient world and overthrow it? Jonah is just a tool in God's hand to bring one of the greatest revivals to one of the most unlikely cities in the ancient world.

---

[58] "Revival," Noah Webster, *Webster's Dictionary: An American Dictionary of the English Language*, 4th Edition (New York: S. Converse Publishing, 1828).

[59] Leonard Ravenhill in Timothy Hill, *Beyond the Mist: A Quest for Authentic Revival* (Branson, MO: Tim Hill Ministries, 2010), 174.

[60] Martyn Lloyd-Jones, *Revival* (Wheaton, IL: Crossway, 1987), 120.

[61] Iain Harnish Murray, *Revival and Revivalism: The Making and Marring of American Evangelicalism, 1750-1858* (Edinburgh etc.: Banner of Truth Trust, 1996), 135.

The City of Nineveh

When Jonah was spit out on the dry land, likely near Joppa where he had begun his run from God. He must have been relieved to be alive. He was back from the dead. This city stood on the eastern bank of the Tigris River.

The Place. He made a beeline for Nineveh around six hundred miles back to where God called him in the first place.

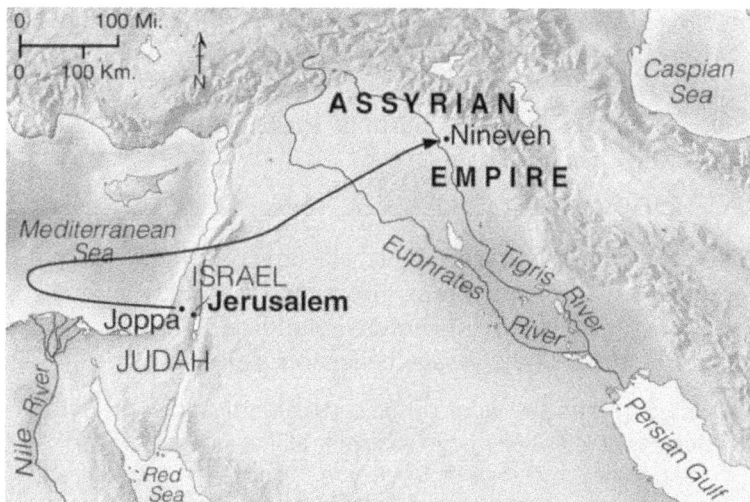

In 1845, a famous British archeologist, Austen Henry Layard discovered ancient Nineveh under the city of modern Mosul, Iraq. The city's towers and massive walls were uncovered. Among the ruins of the city was a vast library consisting of more than 22,000 clay tablets with cuneiform writing detailing 1200 years of history. In 612 B.C., the city of Nineveh would be conquered and burned to the ground by King Nebuchadnezzar of Babylon, but for now, they are given an opportunity to repent.

Protection. Nineveh was incredibly protected. When the archeologists uncovered the walls, they estimated the original walls were 100 feet high and 50 feet thick, and the main wall, interspersed by 15 gates, was over seven and one-half miles long.[62] Of course their army was

---

[62] *International Standard Bible Encyclopedia*, "Nineveh," by T. G. Pinches, 4:2147-51; *Wycliffe Bible Encyclopedia*, "Nineveh," by Elmer B. Smick, 2:1208-10; and *The New Bible Dictionary*, "Nineveh," by D. J. Wiseman, 888-90.

fearsome and legendary in cruelty. Their philosophy of war was to terrorize, humiliate, mutilate, and utterly desolate their enemies. They were the original prototype of a psychopathic terrorist nation.

Population. The total population was probably about 600,000, including the people who lived in the suburbs outside the city walls (*cf* 4:11).

Pagans. Out of all the dark metropolises, Nineveh was one of the darkest. The residents were pagan idolaters and worshipped Asur and Ishtar, the chief male and female deities, as did almost all the Assyrians. No one is deserving of God's free grace, so Jonah's heart was marred, and he had trouble really wanting them to be in God's family. Instead, we should have the burning evangelistic heart of Charles Spurgeon who once prayed:

> Lord, hasten to bring in all thine elect—and then elect some more.[63]

The Power of God. We might ask ourselves today, how do we change and transform our culture? How can we who are so small overcome the hostile atheism, self-centered worldliness, and insane confusion of our culture? God gives us the answer in Jonah 3.

Jonah 3:1-5 | Then the word of the Lord came to Jonah the second time, saying, [2] "Arise, go to Nineveh, that great city, and call out against it the message that I tell you." [3] So Jonah arose and went to Nineveh, according to the word of the Lord. Now Nineveh was an exceedingly great city, three days' journey in breadth. [4] Jonah began to go into the city, going a day's journey. And he called out, "Yet forty days, and Nineveh shall be overthrown!" [5] And the people of Nineveh believed God. They called for a fast and put on sackcloth, from the greatest of them to the least of them.

Key Thought: God desires to give his people revival if his people will dare to ask him for it. Through personal revival, God often brings revival to entire cities and nations. He often sends revival to those who least deserve it.

When God wants to send revival, he often uses the most unlikely people to reach the most unlikely candidates.

---

[63] William Young Fullerton, *Charles Haddon Spurgeon, A Biography* (London: Williams and Norgate Publishers, 1920), 182.

THE PERSON THE SPIRIT USES IN REVIVAL (3:1-4)

God's persistent grace can transform you if you let it. It certainly transformed Jonah. God's grace is what gives us a second chance. If necessary, he will provide us with a third, and a fourth, and so on. God's grace is truly unrelenting!

Jonah wasn't much, but he was a man with a message. Right now, he was a soaking wet mess! Fresh from the fish's belly, Jonah stood on shaky legs, thirsty and hungry, but he was alive. You can imagine Jonah looking around with his heart beating, surveying the Mediterranean Sea for any signs of that great fish. Seeing none, Jonah likely submerged back into the water to wash his face and clothes and body from the blubber and mess of the interior of the great fish. Even with all the scrubbing, we can imagine that Jonah's skin was pale, and his hair bleached white from the gastric acids of the fish's digestive system.

Mustering all the strength he could, Jonah walked on his tender, bare feet a short way up the beach toward Joppa. Jerusalem wasn't far from here. He could very easily just go home, or at least stay in Jerusalem and rest. He just wanted to go home. But before he could contemplate running from God again, the word of the Lord came to Jonah the second time.

Someone Who Hears God's Word

Jonah 3:1-2a | Then the word of the LORD came to Jonah the second time, saying, [2] "Arise, go to Nineveh."

Jonah was prepared for the word. Jonah had been in the belly of the fish for three days and three nights. God's word had been hidden and treasured in his heart. He sang his own psalm to God. Jonah is spit out by the great fish onto dry land, probably in the vicinity of Philistia, near Joppa, where his journey away from God had begun. Suddenly, he hears the word of God!

Jonah was pierced by the word. "Arise, Jonah! Get up and go to Nineveh," came the Lord's gentle but firm voice. God's voice was so much clearer now. Jonah's heart was pierced by the word. You know you are experiencing personal revival when God's voice cuts deep into you.

Jonah was persuaded by the word. There was true fear in his heart when he heard God's voice. His head was bowed. He was a broken man.

He had defied God and lost. He had run from God, but there was no escape from the Lord's reach. God did a mighty work when Jonah was in the belly of the great fish. Now he hears the word of the Lord. Broken, he now obeys. He begins to make his trek to Nineveh, some five hundred and fifty miles away.

I had a Jonah-like experience in the belly of a Ford F-350 as it were. In November 2018, as I was stationary, making a left turn, a Ford F-350 pushed me into oncoming traffic where I was hit again and sustained a traumatic brain injury that laid me up for three months. It was a time of deep wrestling with God for me.

What did God do for me? I was like Jonah in so many ways. I knew the word of God well, but in some ways, I needed to know how to walk in the word like I should have. I knew all the answers, but there were a lot of spiritual walls in my heart that kept my heart filled with the noise of anxiety, which would lead to anger and frustration and even despair at times. I learned that I needed to give up everything except Jesus Christ. God squeezed me in the "belly of the Ford F-350." Jonah was no longer worried about his eloquence or prosperity. He had a personal revival and a renewed walk with God. When we get right with God, we have a new hunger for God's word. We not only experience the glory of the truth, but the power of the Author of the word!

Someone Given Second Chances

God has never used perfect people. The only perfect one was his only Son, Jesus Christ. It seems that through human eyes, Jonah was not just imperfect, but squarely disqualified. He had run from his call. He would rather die than go to Nineveh. But rescued him with a great fish. He set his feet on dry land after three days. If God were to say, "Go home now, Jonah. I am glad you have repented of your disobedience, but you are no longer useful to me," he would be just and reasonable in so doing. But this is not God's way. Thus, instead of reading of God's rejection of Jonah, we find God gives Jonah a second chance.[64]

Jonah 3:1-2a | Then the word of the LORD came to Jonah the second time, saying, [2] "Arise, go to Nineveh."

---

[64] Timothy J. Keller, "The Secret Siege of Nineveh, Jonah 3" from *The Timothy Keller Sermon Archive* (New York City: Redeemer Presbyterian Church, 2013).

Does God always give us a second chance? Does God stoop to use those who have rejected his calling, turned a deaf ear to his word, and pursued a course of determined disobedience? Yes, he is like that. If he did not, none of us could serve him.[65] He gives a second, and third, and forth, and hundredth chances!

God is the God of second chances! God comes back to Jonah and says, "I'm ready to send you to Nineveh." Now that doesn't make any sense. Jonah has let God down. Do you take an officer who has just been court-martialed and immediately give him the command in the most crucial battle of the war? I mean these heroic quests ought to be for the cream of the crop, for the people who had the highest grade point, for the guy who whipped everybody else in the tryouts. You don't give it to Jonah, but God does. In fact, God has this funny habit of doing that.[66] God loves to use people who have been greatly humbled through deep suffering. Jonah was in the belly of a fish. His hard heart had been somewhat softened. He's ready to go, and God says for the second time, "Go…"

Consider Peter. In Matthew 16:17 Jesus refers to Peter as "Simon son of Jonah," which suggests some connection between the apostle and the prophetic protagonist of the book of Jonah.[67] Peter's track record is awful. Who would put this guy in charge of laying the foundation for New Testament Christianity? Why, after Peter's incredible denial of Christ for the third time would the Lord choose him to be chief of the apostles? Like Jonah, it was like Peter died to his call as an apostle. He goes back to his fishing business. I can just hear Peter, "I'm a failure at this apostle thing, but I sure can fish" (*cf* Jn 21:3). But Jesus pursues Peter. He restores Peter and commissions him for Pentecost. Remember? He tells Peter, "Feed my sheep" (*cf* Jn 21:15-19). What we learn from Jonah and Peter and so many others in the Scriptures is that failures make us useful. Fifty days after denying Christ, Peter preaches Pentecost and three thousand are born again!

And what about Abraham? He twice doubted God's protection when he essentially gave his wife to the king's haram—first Pharaoh and then Abimelech. God was gracious and blessed Abraham with

---

[65] Ibid.

[66] Ibid.

[67] Mark Allen Powell, "Echoes of Jonah in the New Testament" (Spring 2007), *Luther Seminary Journal*, Volume 27, No. 2, 158.

riches instead of punishment. Then Abraham and Sarah laughed when they heard they would have a son in their old age. They appropriately named him "Isaac" which means "laughter." This is how amazing God's salvation and grace is that it is so unbelievable it makes you laugh! What an amazing God of second chances.

Someone Willing to Obey

Jonah 3:1-3a | Then the word of the LORD came to Jonah the second time, saying, **²** "Arise, go to Nineveh, that great city, and call out against it the message that I tell you." **³** So Jonah arose and went to Nineveh, according to the word of the LORD.

Jonah had run from God in disobedience. Chastening for him had been so good for him. It brought him to touch the hem of Jesus garment as it were in the belly of the great fish. When God touches you, when you encounter the living God, his word becomes alive. Faith overwhelms you. And it's like electricity overcoming the circuits of a lamppost and what was once dark now shines. The word, now alive, is powerful and unstoppable. Jonah in his flesh despised the Ninevites, but with his view refocused on the Lord, was one of surrender and obedience.

Now, in this moment of surrender, he was willing to do whatever God had for him, even to go to the notorious capital city of the Assyrians, Nineveh.

Jonah was left on the shores of the Mediterranean Sea, perhaps in Joppa near the land of Philistia. He heard God's word, and then he obeyed it. He began a journey of over 550 miles to the city of Nineveh, which today is Mosul, Iraq. It was a long, long journey.

There was a pathway of God's call for Jonah. He was to straight to Nineveh and preach judgment. Jonah is finally listening. God says "go" to his children, and they obey. If they refuse, then comes chastening. We need a fish or a whale of some kind. We need to be swallowed by some monstrous situation. But like Jonah, when we come out of the fish, and we want to obey. The main thing God desires is your obedience. He doesn't need your gift of gab. He doesn't need your mere theological education or your people skills. He wants your heart. Don't be afraid of where he's calling you or what he's calling you to do. Don't let fear take hold of you. Keep your eyes on him and go!

You need to obey God's calling and get out of where you are. Go. Your "going" may be a phone call to encourage someone. For most of us, the going is walking across our neighborhood or even across the church auditorium and asking another family to come over to your home. Be the hands and feet of Jesus. He says, "Bring me your burdens. Bring me your hurts. I will understand." You are to be Jesus to people. That's the point of going.

Someone Called to a Destination

Jonah 3:2-4a | "Arise, go to Nineveh, that great city, and call out against it the message that I tell you." **3** So Jonah arose and went to Nineveh, according to the word of the LORD. Now Nineveh was an exceedingly great city, three days' journey in breadth. **4** Jonah began to go into the city, going a day's journey.

The city's renown. Nineveh was a truly "great city" as we read. Nineveh had great *culture* with great schools and centers of learning.[68] The city had many merchants and shops. There were city gathering places where people enjoyed live music (the only kind they had!) with a variety of instruments like drums, flutes, and harps. They even had sports like wrestling and hunting Aside from the renown of their culture, they were incredible *engineers.* Eighteen different canals have been found that brought water to the Assyrian Empire capital of Nineveh. They invented new forms of irrigation to water crops. The Assyrians were amazing with *mathematics.* They were the first to function on a 60-second minute and a 60-minute hour, which we still use today. They also divided up the circle into 360 degrees. They were among the first to invent longitude and latitude in geographical navigation. They're also renowned for the first truly great *invention*: the wheel! While one wants to re-invent the *wheel*, it was likely invented by the Assyrians, first to create pottery, and then to make the first chariots.[69]

The city's location. Jonah's journey was quite the trek! Five hundred and fifty miles was the distance, and there were no automobiles

---

[68] Joshua J. Mark, "The Neo-Assyrian Empire," *World History Encyclopedia* (Surrey, UK: World History Publishing, 2014), https://www.worldhistory.org/Neo-Assyrian_Empire/.

[69] Jonathan Reich, *Ancient Assyrians: History, Civilization & Culture* (Mountain View, CA: Study.com, 2022), https://study.com/academy/lesson/ancient-assyrians-history-civilization-culture.html

or trains to get there. He might have grabbed a donkey as he walked
through Israel. You can imagine him traveling for several weeks, stop-
ping to eat and rest at times. Maybe he got some gold coins and a good
supply of dried fruit and flasks of water for the journey. We don't know
how he got there. The Bible doesn't say.

The city's wealth. When the ancient city of Nineveh was uncovered,
among the 22,000 cuneiform tablets was the famous "Black Obelisk"
tablet which depicted the incredible luxury of the city with the import
of exotic animals, including camels, monkeys, and rhinoceroses. They
had an incredible array of various foods and clothing from all over the
ancient world. Assyria advanced major trade routes and became the
main trade partners of the ancient world.[70] Remember Jonah is a
prophet from fancy Samaria during a time of great prosperity, during
the reign of Jeroboam II. Archaeological evidence confirms the biblical
account of his reign as the most prosperous that the northern kingdom
of Israel had yet known.[71] Yet Nineveh had even greater riches than Jonah had ever seen in prosperous Israel. Nineveh had luxury with pal-
aces and buildings of unheard-of splendor and gathering places for
amusement. Certainly, Jonah must have preached against these frivol-
ities.

The city's size. We read that Jonah traveled a day's journey into the
city, about twenty miles. Nineveh was the greatest and largest city the
world had yet seen up to that time. Including the suburbs of Nineveh,
we read that in order to walk through the city, it took three days. Nineveh had the *diameter* of a three-day journey, where one day equals
about 20 miles. This was a city 60 miles in diameter, which is about the
size of Chicago and all the suburbs, what we call Chicagoland. It was an
impregnable fortress. This was a city with military might, economic so-
phistication, and cultural reputation.

The city's logo. The city of Nineveh literally means "Fish City." In
ancient times, when you wrote out the name "Nineveh," you would use
cuneiform for *Ninâ* which means "fish." Nine-veh means "the place of
the fish" or literally "Fish City." The infamous Nimrod was the founder
of Nineveh. They worshipped Dagon, the fish god, like the Philistines.

---

[70] Salvatore Gaspa, "Textiles in the Neo-Assyrian Empire," January 1, 2018,
https://doi.org/10.1515/9781501503054.

[71] M. Broshi, I. Finkelstein, (1992). "The Population of Palestine in Iron Age
II", *Bulletin of the American School of Oriental Research*, 287: 47–60.

So God sends them a prophet who is vomited out of a fish to preach to Fish City! He smells like a fish. Talk about contextualization!

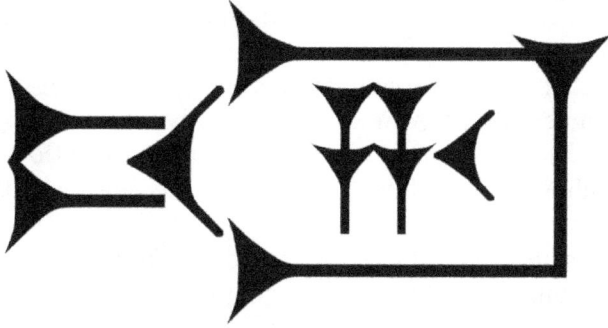

"Nineveh" in neo-Assyrian cuneiform, and then in simplified cuneiform

The city's walls. Nineveh had walls 100 feet high and 50-feet thick, and the main one, which had by 15 gates, was over seven and one-half miles long. This was an impenetrable city, yet here comes Jonah with the same power that Moses had when he took on the armies of Pharaoh.

Nineveh's massive walls

The city's army. The Assyrian army had the most highly advanced military technology of their time with horses and chariots with iron wheels, spears and iron swords, daggers, javelins, and slings, and dev-astating fiery arrows from their trained marksmen. The cavalry was so large that many units had up to a thousand horsemen. The Assyrians were notoriously cruel and without mercy. The prophet Hosea was a younger contemporary of Jonah, and his prophecies had begun to warn Israel that unless they repented, they would be conquered by the Assyrians. Not only that, but the Assyrians' cruelty was also incomprehensible, killing women, children, and innocents along with the cruelest tortures ever devised.

The city's impassability. In the Lord of the Rings, Nobody in their right mind would even think of besieging the city, let alone trying to capture the city, because you couldn't even get an army around it. Who had an army that could stretch around the circumference of this city? But the foolishness of God is wiser than the wisdom of men, and God decides, not just to besiege the city, but to sack it with an army of one.

The city's people though cultured were idol worshippers. To Israel, they were the untouchables. They were utterly pagan. Who are the untouchables today that God wants to save? God has a heart to reach those raised in extremist Muslim nations. Are you afraid of that? God has a heart to reach the mentally ill. Who are the untouchables today? God saves people with criminal records all the time.

The Ninevites are the most unlikely candidates for a spiritual revival. They ruled with a gruesome tyranny. Archeological records show that they maimed and tortured their captives and seem to revel in bloody butchery. The prophet Nahum (3:1-4) describes the city as "the beautiful and faithless city; mistress of deadly charms, enticed the nations with her beauty. She taught them all her magic, enchanting people everywhere." Morally, the Ninevites were corrupt. Spiritually, they were in pitch-blackness. Think of ISIS in the Middle East or Boko Haram in Nigeria – but worse and pagan.

We are to lay down our lives for sinners, even notorious ones. God sent Jesus into this world not to serve himself, but to serve others and lay down his life as a sacrifice for many. That has to be our commitment and calling as well.

Someone with God's Message

Jonah's message wasn't "God loves you and has a great plan for your life." His message was "Repent, Yahweh will no longer tolerate your sin."

Jonah 3:4 | Jonah began to go into the city, going a day's journey. And he called out, "Yet forty days, and Nineveh shall be overthrown!"

A message of warning. God's call to Jonah was to preach judgment to a place he never dreamed of going. He was to preach exactly what God told him to preach. God's messengers are never to edit the message. We are to be the mailmen. "Forty days and judgment will be delivered!" This wasn't the Roman's Road. This was really a call from God's prophet to warn these brutal people that God's judgment was about to fall. There were no qualifiers, like if you repent, I will relent. None of that. It was straight up judgment. Jonah was likely glad to preach that. He didn't want to preach God's unrelenting love to Nineveh. Only judgment. Yet God does love Nineveh. They have heard enough about this awesome God who brought a mixed multitude out of Egypt. "Surely if he loved the Egyptians he will love us too," they must have thought.

It's not rude to tell the gospel to someone. It's merciful. When I was a child, I grew up swimming in the swampland of Louisiana. Our home was right on the Tickfaw River which eventually leads to Lake Ponchatrain and the Gulf of Mexico. It wasn't very often, but every once in a while, someone would spot these highly poisonous snakes, water moccasins, slithering on the surface of the river. Immediately someone would yell, "Snake!" and all would retreat to the shoreline. Was it rude or ill-mannered or disrespectful to give that warning to all? No, in fact, to not give it would be unloving. Some saw the snake, but all heard the warning.

That's how Jonah felt. He had just come from being in the belly of another sea creature, and he gave the warning. He couldn't make them see the "snake" of their sin. That's the Holy Spirit's role. The Spirit is the agent of conviction and illumination. Jonah knew what it was like to be "buried" in the consequences of his own sin when he was in the belly of the fish. Now he was calling out with conviction for these Ninevite sinners to find the same deliverance he found.

A message of salvation. It's not about the messenger. It's the gospel that saves people. Somebody says, "I'm not articulate. I don't know what to say. It's easy for you to say. You're articulate. You're well-trained." Look at Jonah! Jonah had a message of judgment. He wasn't trying to impress anyone. He likely secretly hoped they perished. Yet Jonah changed the city.

They said of Paul: "He's not articulate." They said of Paul: "His letters are weighty and strong, but his bodily presence is weak, and his speech of no account" (2 Cor 10:10). Moses said, "I can't talk; I'm slow of speech" (Exo 4:10). The greatest of God's messengers were not much to listen to. It's not about the power of fancy speech but of the presence of God falling on the people. Paul gives us the secret of evangelism. It's not a slick presentation but a supernatural message. Paul was clear about the power of the gospel.

> Romans 1:16 | For I am not ashamed of the gospel, for it is the power of God for salvation to everyone who believes, to the Jew first and also to the Greek.

God is not impressed with slick messengers. If God used a donkey to speak to someone (*cf* Num 22:21-39), then God can surely use a reluctant prophet to bring about a great revival with wide-reaching salvation.

Like Jonah, God sent Paul into the city. All of the Roman Empire was changed by a bunch of slaves and street people. How could that have happened? How did Christians actually, literally take over the Roman Empire? It's because Paul did not trust in eloquence, but in the power of God.

Did you see what he said? He got up and said, "Forty more days and Nineveh will be overturned." Do you call that a good message? He didn't even tell them to repent! He didn't even tell them there was possibility of escape. This seemed like an impossible message, but God changed the whole country through him. Lift up your voice. Open your heart. God is ready to save those around you. He's not depending on your great articulation, of your perfect preparedness, or your power of persuasion. God is ready to use you in spite of you. The power of God is in his message of mercy and his agent of salvation, the Holy Spirit who regenerates the stone-cold hearts of sinners and gives the new, living hearts of flesh.

THE PEOPLE THE SPIRIT TOUCHES IN REVIVAL (3:5-9)

Jonah 3:5-6 | And the people of Nineveh believed God. They called for a fast and put on sackcloth, from the greatest of them to the least of them. [6] The word reached the king of Nineveh, and he arose from his throne, removed his robe, covered himself with sackcloth, and sat in ashes.

What a statement. The people Nineveh believed God. A great many turned to God in true faith. Every urban planter, every sociologist, every politician, every counselor, and every social worker wants this to happen. "If only the people of the city would turn from their evil ways and their violence, so we'd be done with the oppression, crime, racism, and all of the problems of the city." How did Jonah have such success? Jonah's message was so powerful and successful not because of his eloquence, but because God granted repentance. God brought the people to repentance, and he sent a Holy Spirit empowered revival to Nineveh.

How do we engage pagan, idol-filled people? People in the great cities of the world live relentless lives, consumed with our immediate concerns: running a business, raising a family, and enjoying some sport. Jonah walked into the intense activity of a large city and said, "Forty more days and Nineveh will be overturned." Authentic gospel preaching always engages people with eternal issues. It lifts our horizons from the immediate interests of our lives to the imminent and overwhelming reality of eternal life or everlasting destruction.[72]

Touched with Faith

Jonah 3:5a | And the people of Nineveh believed God.

What an amazing historical record! This verse reminds me of the great patriarch Abraham.

Romans 4:3 | Abraham believed God, and it was counted to him as righteousness.

Biblical faith. These pagans had to be taught about the one true and living God, Yahweh. And just as Abraham was made righteous by being illuminated about the living God and by trusting and clinging to him as his Savior, so the Ninevites came to know the Lord by grace through faith. Jonah reports that the people came to believe God. They believed God's word that judgment was coming. It was through his word that God opened the eyes of the Ninevites.

Romans 10:17 | Faith comes by hearing, and hearing by the word of Christ.

---

[72] C. Smith, *Jonah*, 3:4.

People in ancient times were saved the same way we are saved to-day: by grace through faith. Jonah preached. Of course, we don't know all he said. So much of the narratives are abbreviated. Not much is recorded of what he preached. "Forty days" and then Nineveh is gone (4:4). I'm pretty sure that's Jonah's sermon title. And when God saw that they turned away from their wicked way, God "had compassion and did not bring upon them the destruction he had threatened"

Unexpected faith. That morning for them began like any other day. Who knew that the most cruel pagans of history would turn to the living God? They had no awareness of their spiritual state. They were dead in trespasses and sins. They knew nothing of God's divine cloud of judgment upon them. Suddenly through Jonah's words, they had a flood of light shining in their hearts with alarming power. God's judgment was looming over their heads. They could no longer comfortable with the state of things. They could not think of this little prophet in front of them in natural terms. Instead, all they could feel was the presence of God with divine justice about to fall in forty days. They were no longer asleep and dead in their sin but crying out to God for mercy. They who had been such notorious sinners were calling out to God with their own version of the sinner's prayer, "God, be merciful to me a sinner" (Lk 18:13).

Divine faith. Jesus teaches us that this faith and illumination is the work of the Holy Spirit (Jn 16:8-11). Jonah's mission was the same as the apostle Paul's. He was sent to "open the eyes of the Gentiles" (Acts 26:17-18). How did their eyes open? How did the ancient revival of Nineveh occur? God was drawing them. Remember the words of Jesus.

John 6:44 | No one can come to me unless the Father who sent me draws him.

God drew them through national suffering. God drew them through *massive national suffering.* Historians have pointed out that about the time of Jonah's mission, Assyria had experienced a series of famines, plagues, revolts, and eclipses, all of which were seen as harbingers of far worse things to come. Some have argued that this was God's way of preparing the ground for Jonah.[73] When things get dark in our life and we are crushed, it is often the time that God was working. He worked in Jonah. He was now working in Nineveh.

---

[73] Keller, *Rediscovering Jonah*, 85.

God drew them through national monotheism. God drew them through *national monotheism.* Scholars who have studied Assyrian history have suggested possible reasons for this response. Under King Adad-Nirari III (c. 810–783 B.C.) the Assyrians had begun a trend toward monotheism. And just before the probable time of Jonah's arrival, a great plague had marked the reign of King Assurdan II (c. 771–754 B.C.). During this time there was a plaque erected that said:

Trust in the one God [Nebo]: do not trust in any other god.[74]—*Ancient Stone Plaque in Nineveh*

God drew them through national mourning. Whatever the contributing factors, the Assyrians did respond to God's messenger. King, nobles, and slaves fasted, mourned, and prayed, humbling themselves before God.[75] But what are the contributing factors to real revival and awakening? We can see right here in the glorious revival in Nineveh what those factors are.

With the king's repentance, it looks like God had been drawing him. From historical records, that King Assurdan II was already seeking the Lord. Jonah came in and confirmed what God was already doing. This king later, in his joy of finally knowing God, makes a decree for all under his authority to worship Yahweh, the one true and living God (3:7-9). Do you believe that God is drawing unlikely people to himself? Open your mouth and be bold in evangelism, and you will see! The Ninevites believed God!

The Welsh revival. When the word of God went sweeping through Wales in the early 1900s, God gave a tremendous revival, and approximately 70,000 came to faith in Christ in the first two months and over 100,000 during the course of the revival. People would gather at the churches, sometimes hundreds at a time, in the middle of the night. Time stopped during the revival. People would run into the meetings crying out, "Is there mercy for me?" There were tremendous labor union problems that were happening inside the mines. When the revival came, they were wiped away, because on company time, the managers started to sponsor Bible studies, and the bosses and the miners were all

[74] Heffron Yağmur et al., *At the Dawn of History Ancient Near Eastern Studies in Honor of J.N. Postgate* (Winona Lake, IN: Eisenbrauns, 2017), 459.
[75] Lawrence O. Richards, *The Teacher's Commentary* (Wheaton, IL: Victor Books, 1987), 472.

part of the Bible studies. Revival broke out. The miners began to bring back all the things they had been stealing. Do you know how all mines had one shed where the company kept its tools, and you used the tools? Miners had been stealing them for years. During the revival, they had to build five new sheds at most mines just to put back all the tools the miners started bringing back![76]

Give yourself to the Holy Spirit right now. Don't be afraid. He's taking you to the full joy of holiness. Let his word penetrate your soul and cut your spirit. In a widespread way, and on a massive scale, this took place in Nineveh. It continues to take place through the ministry of God's word today. [77]

Touched with God's Calling

Jonah 3:5b | They called for a fast and put on sackcloth, from the greatest of them to the least of them.

The king of Nineveh, who was the greatest among the people, was being called by the living God.

Psalm 110:3a | Your people will offer themselves freely on the day of your power, in holy garments.

In response to God's call, the king took off his royal robes, and he put on the rough fabric of sackcloth. He was mourning for his own sin. The people of Nineveh followed the king's example and began to mourn for their sins with fasting and sackcloth. In the Bible, sackcloth, and ashes was worn as a sign of repentance for sin. Simply put, sackcloth and ashes were an external demonstration of an internal condition. It's like saying, "I deserve hell, and I'm begging you God for mercy." It was a visible mark of someone's deep sorrow and mourning. The action itself required a most sincere humility that only the repentant one can possess. It was a also a sign that they were seeking God's forgiveness for what they had done. There was hope for mercy and grace. Notice everyone, from the greatest (like the king of Nineveh) to the least of them, heard and responded to God's call. What would it look like in your neighborhood and your city if everyone, from the least to the greatest responded to God's call?

---

[76] *Cf* David Matthews, *I Saw the Welsh Revival: An Account of the 1904 Revival in Wales* (Goshen, IN: Pioneer Books, 1992).

[77] Ferguson, *Man Overboard*, 71.

Touched with Repentance

The Ninevites believed God. They responded to God's call. And now we see that they repented from their heart. Repentance is literally "a change of mind." It means to see things as God sees them. To now love what God loves and hate what God hates. Repentance is a gift of God. God must grant us eyes to see, like Lydia from the Philippian church. God opened the eyes of Lydia (Acts 16:14). That's repentance.

> **Jonah 3:6-9** | The word reached the king of Nineveh, and he arose from his throne, removed his robe, covered himself with sack-cloth, and sat in ashes. [7] And he issued a proclamation and published through Nineveh, "By the decree of the king and his nobles: Let neither man nor beast, herd nor flock, taste anything. Let them not feed or drink water, [8] but let man and beast be covered with sackcloth, and let them call out mightily to God. Let everyone turn from his evil way and from the violence that is in his hands. [9] Who knows? God may turn and relent and turn from his fierce anger, so that we may not perish."

The king turned from his evil ways and demonstrated true repentance by covering himself with sackcloth and sat in ashes while he fasted from food and water. He made a proclamation that all the people and even the animals were to join him. He wanted them to "call out mightily to God." Wow. Wherever revival comes there is a radical awakening to the presence of God is felt and responding to his presence is vastly more important than food, water, or comfort. The soul cries out for a taste of the divine mercy and comforting presence.

One of the beautiful events we witness in this ancient revival is how God uses the repentance of the king of Nineveh to spark this awakening. Who is this king? The king of Assyria had his home at times at Nineveh (2 Kgs 19:36; Isa 37:37). It could be the actual king of Assyria, or perhaps a provincial governor. Whatever the king's identity, he humbled himself and begged that God would "turn and relent" from his judgment "so that we might not perish." The king is really the key to the entire revival. Here is the greatest revival in the Old Testament in a pagan nation. It's absolutely incredible. When Jonah preached, the king was already eager and prepared, and he led the way. He made a citywide decree: "Worship the Lord with fasting and repentance. Turn from your violence and turn to the Lord. He may in mercy save us." And that's exactly what God did.

God sent me to Louisiana recently. I was there for the Mecca to Christ International conference in Alexandria. But while I was there, I met a childhood friend named Trey Harris. He has been a believer for only eight months. The first thing he did was gather 75 men to help these hurting men with the love of Christ. He gathered three pastors from three different churches to minister to these men. Trey is a man of influence in a smaller community who people follow. He is using that influence for Christ. How am I using my influence for Christ? How are you, like the king of Nineveh, influencing others so they might repent and come to Jesus?

THE PATIENCE GOD DEMONSTRATES IN REVIVAL (3:10)

Jonah 3:10 | God saw what they did, how they turned from their evil way, God relented of the disaster that he had said he would do to them, and he did not do it.

The same God who saved the Ninevites extends his mercy to us today. They didn't deserve it.

Divine Judgment

Jonah 3:10a | God saw what they did.

All people on the earth deserve divine judgment. The God who saw their repentance had also seen their wicked sin. It says that it ascended to him in heaven. Their sins were so great, God had to do something about it. He would either destroy them through judgment or redeem them through mercy. They had to choose, and they chose repentance.

Divine Mercy

Jonah 3:10 | God saw what they did, how they turned from their evil way, God relented of the disaster that he had said he would do to them, and he did not do it.

The Ninevites repented. What a way to overthrow the city of Nineveh! They turned with their whole hearts to God. God responded. God overthrew Egypt in judgment by destroying Pharaoh's army with the Red Sea. With Nineveh, he overthrows the city in mercy.

Whoever comes to Jesus will never be cast out. Come without money and without price (Isa 55:1). Come and drink of the wells of salvation. Kings and mighty men, come. Poor and broken, come. Come in humility and drink deeply of the well of salvation. All who are weary and heavy laden with sin, come (Mt 11:28)! And if you come, you will not be disappointed. The gospel is the power of God unto salvation for anyone and everyone who believes (Rom 1:16). Jesus is mighty to save.

Whoever comes in faith, trusting in the Lord will not be disappointed. God relented of the disaster he had for the Ninevites. Why? They demonstrated repentant faith by turning from their evil way with humility. Come to Jesus while you can. For those who will not repent at the preaching of Jesus' death and resurrection, there is greater judgment, for God will call the Ninevites as witnesses on the day of judgment against anyone who rejects the gospel.

> *Matthew 12:41* | The men of Nineveh will rise up at the judgment with this generation and condemn it, for they repented at the preaching of Jonah, and behold, something greater than Jonah is here.

Tremble at what God can do for wicked sinners. Realize he could condemn you, but he chooses to love you. What will you do with that love? Will you repent, if you haven't already, at the preaching of the gospel? Jesus died and rose again for you. Repent and trust him now.

Conclusion

How do you overthrow a world power? No human being can, but God can. This kind of manifest power of God in revival happens individually and it can happen nationally. The Spirit can and has fallen on whole towns and cities and nations even in the recent past. And he falls regularly, suddenly, and shockingly at times in the lives of individuals. We can shout with Jonah, "Salvation is of the Lord!" Jonah is the most unlikely candidate for a preacher of revival. God uses unlikely candidates.

How do you overthrow the human heart? You start with your own personal revival. Start reaching out to the lost in your own sphere of influence. The lost cannot hear without a preacher. We must go with the word of God. The greatest place of weakness is that we won't go. We are like Jonah, comfortable. We like preaching to ourselves. We must see people like Jesus did. He left his comfort zone and came to this earth and died on a lonely cross.

Recently I had the exciting opportunity to go wild hog hunting in Louisiana. There are so many hogs doing mischief that there is no limit to the hunting season. You can capture as many hogs as possible, and the season is all year round. So, there we were, eighty people in total covering 80 acres. It was quite a strange sight. There were about 15 people on horses, 5 four wheelers, and 2 tractors with about 30 people on each hayride.

All in all, we caught 3 hogs. It's pretty hard to catch a hog with a rope. With 80 people, we were able to only get three. It was exhilarating to chase them and to see those on horses who roped the hogs. I don't know about you, but I've never seen a wild hog up close. A big man took down the hog and sat on it. They he'd grab his legs and hog tie it until it settled down. Then they'd bring a cage with water in the bottom, and the hog delighted to get into the cage and cool down. The point is we got excited about catching wild hogs. Maybe that's not your thing, but you'll chase after a sport's team. You'll chase hard after your hobbies, your kids' activities, and the fun things you like. All that is fine. But what about the souls of the lost? Will you pursue them? Oh that God would give us the deep desire to pursue the lost with God's love and heart and compassion.

5 | JONAH 4
THE WORST MISSIONARY IN THE WORLD

O Lord, is not this what I said when I was yet in my country? That is why I made haste to flee to Tarshish; for I knew that you are a gracious God and merciful, slow to anger and abounding in steadfast love, and relenting from disaster. Therefore now, O Lord, please take my life from me, for it is better for me to die than to live.
JONAH 4:2-3

For fifteen years Jim Fixx, author of the bestseller, *The Complete Book of Running*, ran eighty miles a week. He appeared to be in tip-top shape. It didn't seem possible that a man his age could be in better condition. Yet at age fifty-two Fixx died of a massive heart attack while running alone on a Vermont road. His wife, Alice, later said she was certain that Fixx had no idea he suffered from a heart problem. Why? Because he refused to get regular checkups. After Jim Fixx's death, doctors speculated that his heart was so strong he may not have had the telltale chest pains or shortness of breath that usually signal arterial heart disease.[78]

---

[78] Jane Gross, "James F. Fixx Dies Jogging; Author on Running was 52." *The New York Times*, (July 22, 1984), https://www.nytimes.com/1984/07/22/obituaries/james-f-fixx-dies-jogging-author-on-running-was-52.html.

Jonah was one of those people who had everything going for him. He had great theology. He lived in prosperity. He heard from God regularly. But he didn't see his own pride. He was self-deceived. He was glad he was forgiven and redeemed by the Lord, but that's where it ended. His idol was earthly comfort. Sadly, we find that his three-night stay in the great fish didn't strip him of his idolatry.

I doubt if there ever has been a story of God's dealings with undeserving pagans that should give more cause for rejoicing than the story of Jonah. Yet Jonah gets mad at God. Jonah could be called the worst missionary in the history of the world. God used him to bring the greatest revival in the Old Testament to the baddest people in the ancient world, and he's not rejoicing. He's angry. He is the best illustration who ever lived of a man who did exactly what he wasn't supposed to do, who refused to do what God had called him to do. And when he did fulfill God's call, he was angry with God saving the people in Nineveh.

Of all the books of the Bible, Jonah has the most unexpected and shocking final chapter. Most people have heard the story of Jonah, but they think of it as ending at Jonah's repentance and release from the fish. A smaller number of people may be able to tell you that the story goes on and that Jonah went and preached successfully to Nineveh. Almost everyone thinks the story ends right there. Yet there is a final, startling chapter in which the real lessons of the entire narrative are revealed.[79]

It's not unusual that Jonah doesn't want to go to the city most notorious for cruelty. But when God brings revival, he's angry! That's a surprise. If there had ever been a cause for rejoicing, now was the time. He sees one of the most profound revivals in the history of the world break out. We should expect Jonah himself to be literally leaping with joy and thanksgiving. Instead, we find Jonah in the worst "blue funk" imaginable. In fact, he was angry about what had happened, violently angry. He was angry with God.[80]

For many years, I used to scratch my head about Jonah's reaction to this astonishing awakening in Nineveh. Jonah angry? Why? How? Doesn't he understand the mercy of God? But then it hit me. I'm Jonah.

---

[79] Timothy Keller, *Rediscovering Jonah* (New York: Penguin Publishing Group, 2018), 97-98.
[80] Ibid.

Jonah has a sin problem that keeps reappearing. Anger is often an outward symptom of an underlying idol.

Jonah thinks he knows better than God. He's full of pride in himself and unbelief in God. That's the recipe for the deadness of backsliding.

We are often like Jonah. Self-righteous. Filled with knowledge in the head but not the heart. Rules without relationship. We want to choose those who are worthy of saving. Jonah is a prophet, and he needs to grow in God's grace. As we see Jonah, let us exalt and worship the God who can break our hard hearts for the lost.

THE POISON OF ANGER (3:10; 4:1-3)

When we consider why Jonah is such a bad missionary, we have to dig into his heart. He's going to preach against the world's greatest idolators and sinners, but he doesn't realize he's an idolator himself. The poison of anger has infected his life.

Sinful, self-centered anger is a massive idol indicator. What makes you mad when you don't have it? What makes you sad when you don't get it? What makes you despair? What makes you want to escape into foolish thinking? These are the **X-ray questions** that reveal what we are actually worshipping.

Anger Keeps Us Paralyzed

Anger is like a paralytic drug that keeps you unable to move spiritually. Anger fed Jonah's prejudice, and it stopped him from following God's call the first time. His anger from prejudice paralyzed him from caring about the salvation of the world. They were just *too bad* to be saved. Jonah didn't want the Ninevites to repent. He wanted them to burn up like Sodom. But God saw the repentant hearts of the Ninevites and showed mercy.

Jonah 3:10-4:1 | When God saw what they did, how they turned from their evil way, God relented of the disaster that he had said he would do to them, and he did not do it. [1] But it displeased Jonah exceedingly, and he was angry.

Jonah is *gob smacked*. As the prophet Jonah waited the 40 days, he was sure God would still carry out his judgment. Remember, "40 days and Nineveh is done for!" Those 40 days came and went, but God's wrath did not consume Nineveh. He did not treat them like Sodom and Gomorrah before. The text says simply and beautifully: "God relented of the disaster" he had planned. God is focused on *salvation*. Jonah is focused on *retaliation*. For Jonah, this was an injustice of highest proportions. Jonah's self-righteous anger makes him see himself as more righteous than God. Jonah was hurt because his nation and perhaps his own family had been hurt by the dreaded Assyrians. This would be like saving Osama bin Laden a month after 9/11. Would you want to forgive him? Would you want to worship with him?

Anger paralyzes us. Bitterness can overtake us and keep us from thinking at all rationally. We see it in Jonah, but we see it in ourselves.

Satan has a bag of tricks to torture you with the pain of bitterness and anger. It's so bad once you get stuck in it, it's hard to get out. Such pain from bitterness is engineered by Satan to attempt to bind and paralyze you through sin. You respond to a sin against you with sin against your offender. The offenses are real and hurtful, but they are not unforgiveable. The most common offenses can infect your heart with the poison of bitterness.

A broken promise. Do you still remember a broken promise? Have you forgiven the person who broke it?

A broken confidence. If someone has betrayed your confidence, how have you responded?

Personal rejection. This includes not only verbal and emotional rejection but slander and gossip as well. Someone may mean well, but it feels like a criticism. This will make you bitter if you don't deal with it.

False accusation. Being charged falsely with wrongdoing can hurt your reputation and damage relationships. It is difficult to forgive the accuser and restore trust.

Abuse. Physical violence can hurt long after the bruises heal. Sexual abuse can torment much longer than the event that harmed you. Verbal abuse often leaves enduring emotional scars. God, however, can bring healing and give you the supernatural ability to forgive the abuser.[81]

If you find yourself upset and playing the thoughts of your hurt toward someone over and over again, you are already trapped and tied up by bitterness.

This is why we as believers must at all times "walk in the Spirit" for it is then we will not gratify the desires, the urges, the compulsions of

---

[81] Erwin W. Lutzer, *When You've Been Wronged: Moving from Bitterness to Forgiveness* (Chicago, IL: Moody Publishers, 2007).

the flesh (Gal 5:16). Walk in the fruit of the Spirit. You can't be filled with *love, joy, peace, patience*, etc., and be filled with anger and vitriol. Jonah was gratifying his selfish desire that those who hurt him would hurt. He was good and angry, but that was not good. In fact, when we look at it, it's confusing at first.

Anybody who is following this story along would expect there to have just been a Jonah 3:10, and that should've said, "And Jonah returned to his own land rejoicing." But instead, we have a Jonah 4:1 that says, "But it displeased Jonah exceedingly, and he was angry." And we learn that he's angry enough to die. Come on!

What is it that is paralyzing you? Is your heart freed from anger and bitterness? Look at what it did to Jonah. But anger doesn't just keep you *paralyzed*. It keeps you *pouting*.

Anger Keeps Us Pouting

Look at Jonah's prayer. It's actually not much of a prayer. It's a pout! Anger turns your praying into pouting.

> **Jonah 4:2** | And he prayed to the LORD and said, "O LORD, is not this what I said when I was yet in my country? That is why I made haste to flee to Tarshish; for I knew that you are a gracious God and merciful, slow to anger and abounding in steadfast love, and relenting from disaster.

Jonah is beside himself in bitterness. He prays, but he prays wrongly, thinking God is wrong. Anger has blinded Jonah. That's what sin does to any individual. Whenever we allow any sin, especially anger, to enter in, we are giving Satan control over us. We become his marionette. Paul tells us never to be sinfully angry because it is then that we give a place at the table of our heart and mind for the devil to counsel us (Eph 4:26-27). Anger says, "I am a god. I will control this situation. I call the shots." Anger lives and grows in the soil of pride and rebellion. In Hebrews we read something important about bitterness.

> *Hebrews 12:15, NIV* | See to it that no one misses the grace of God and that no bitter root grows up to cause trouble and defile many.

This verse teaches us two things about bitterness: First, it has a root-some source of human pride that causes you not to believe the promises of God; and second, as the root spreads, it defiles many. It blows up into pouting. It starts with pouting to God, but then to others.

Satan squeezes us with bitterness and despair, and we pop with complaints and gossiping that defile many. Instead of covering with love complain with loathing.

Pouting is Self-Righteous

Jonah thought he was right, and he wanted to inform God.

Jonah 4:2a | And he prayed to the LORD and said, "O LORD, is not this what I said when I was yet in my country? That is why I made haste to flee to Tarshish."

We don't specifically know the root of Jonah's anger toward the Ninevites, but it is not hard to imagine. The stories he's heard about these terrorists make him boil. As a prophet of Israel, ministering to God's people, surely he has wept with numbers of broken hearted parents and counseled countless orphaned children. The viciousness and violence of the soldiers. The arrogance of their paganism. I mean Israel is astray, but the Assyrians are on another level! They're monsters. You know that a depth of crippling pride had entered our hearts when we believe we are more righteous than God himself. That was Jonah. He thought he saw things more clearly than God. At the root of all bitterness is unbelief and pride. Jonah thought he knew more about righteousness than God.

Pouting is Self-Serving

Jonah reveals something far more sinister about bitterness. At the heart of bitterness is a satanic thirst to take the throne of God. "God's just too soft! I'd be a better cosmic ruler than him!" Jonah wanted a God who was more like himself, made in Jonah's image.

Jonah 4:2b | "For I knew that you are a gracious God and merciful, slow to anger and abounding in steadfast love, and relenting from disaster."

It's clear that Jonah's not preaching the glories of our merciful God. Instead, he's complaining that God is not more like man. Jonah would like a God who is as petulant as he is.

Jonah knows the attributes of God. God is sovereign. Gracious. Merciful. Slow to anger. Abounding in covenantal love (*hesed*). God is loyal to unworthy sinners. His attitude is self-serving. Jonah knows

God but doesn't like him. God's too soft! Jonah is mad that God is such a God of grace.

When you are pouting, you can't stop it without surrendering to God. Pouting indicates that self is at the center of your life, to the point you feel constrained by your sociopathic flesh to question the living God. It's satanic.

Pouting is Self-Exalting

Jonah 4:2c | "And abounding in steadfast love, and relenting from disaster."

It's important to realize that sinful anger leads to a pouting that is self-exalting. Your flesh is "in it to win it" at all costs. The motive of this angry pouting is not a steadfast love for others, like God demonstrates, but a steadfast commitment to self at all costs, like the devil himself demonstrates.

Jonah is glad that God is gracious, "abounding in hesed" toward Israel. But why is God loyal in his love toward the evil Assyrians?! Jonah is not only self-righteous and self-serving, but he's racist and self-exalting as well.

We all know that Jonah in his complaining is quoting God's description of himself to Moses in Exodus 34:6. Why would a preacher get exceedingly angry when, as a response to his preaching, he actually turns a culture away from violence, oppression, and wickedness to the living God?[82] I'll tell you why. He's blinded by thinking his dung doesn't stink. We all know we are sinners but come on. There's sin, and then there's really bad sin. Jonah basically says in verse 2, "God, I do not understand how your love operates. I don't get it. It doesn't make sense to me." God sets out in this chapter to teach Jonah how his love operates, so the whole chapter is about love, and the incredible collapse of Jonah is because of a misunderstanding of God's love.[83]

When self is on the throne of your life, the bitterness, complaining, unrelenting thoughts, and the fighting, bickering, and ugliness will never end. As long as your pride is ruling you, your pouting will continue and keep going. It cannot be reasoned with. It must be crucified (Gal 2:20).

---

[82] Timothy J. Keller, "Abounding in Love, Jonah 4:1-11" from *The Timothy Keller Sermon Archive* (New York City: Redeemer Presbyterian Church, 2013).
[83] Ibid.

God's Patience in Our Pouting

The only thing keeping Jonah from oblivion at this point is the patience of God. It's ironic because this patient love of God is seen in four situations: Jonah running in chapter 1, the sailors in chapter 1, the Ninevites in chapter 3, and Jonah's pouting in chapter 4.

The key teaching in this passage is that fruitful, prominent Christians can fall back into old patterns of sin and self-deception so that only the patient love of God stands between us and oblivion. God's patient love is such that he will always bring us back. We are directly taught in the New Testament that Christians are predestined to be conformed to the image of Christ (Rom 8:29). Do Christians stumble and fall yes—but not permanently. We're taught about the patient love of God here because Jonah is a perfect example. We should not point our finger at Jonah and be surprised. We should look in the mirror and see that we are Jonah.

Do you think that those old patterns of anger, and of fear, and of dishonesty, and denial are all gone away? Have all those bad habit patterns vanished? No. They're under a death sentence, but they're still there. You have to crucify them every day. The condemning power of sin is gone forever, but the actual power of sin, though under a death sentence, is still present. Therefore, it can erupt.[84]

The moment you stop walking in the Spirit and give into your flesh, you can become as blinded to the love of God as Jonah was. The fact that we are shocked by this passage shows how used to our own blindness we have become. Indeed, God "is patient with you, not wanting anyone to perish, but everyone to come to repentance" (2 Pet 3:9).

Anger Keeps Us in Pain

Jonah 4:3 | Therefore now, O LORD, please take my life from me, for it is better for me to die than to live.

Anger can be so petulant that it renders the one who drinks it in hopeless. You become so blinded by anger you experience despair. You just want to die. That was Jonah. A prophet no less. He knows God's word. He's just quoted Moses in Exodus 34:6. That's the Old Testament version of our Ephesians 2:8-9. Salvation is by grace through faith. The Ninevites came by grace. They believed God (3:1). Miracle of miracles.

---

[84] Ibid.

But Jonah can't see it and certainly cannot appreciate it. That's what anger will do to a person. Anger can ultimately lead a person to want to die and to even take their own life. Jonah of course was merely asking for God to take his life. "God, why didn't you just kill me, and leave me at the bottom of the Mediterranean? Why do I have to see my mortal enemies brought into your kingdom? I like my worship free from Assyrians. I don't want to worship with those monsters."

This reminds me of a story from Corrie Ten Boom. During World War II, she and her sister Betsie had been sent to a German prison camp for the crime of helping Jews in Holland. Her precious Betsie died in the camp. Corrie lived, and after the war began to teach and speak everywhere of God's forgiveness for everyone. Shortly after the war God called Corrie to testify in Germany. Corrie told the people of the love, forgiveness and healing that God wanted to bring to Germany.

During one meeting a former Nazi prison officer approached Corrie. He had been one of the very guards who had abused and neglected her and her sister in prison. He did not recognize her, but she recognized him. He had become a Christian, and now asked Corrie if she could forgive him. Corrie was shocked! She now recognized him! Could she forgive him?

At first Corrie resisted, but then with the strength God gave her, she was able to hold her hand out to the man, and tell him: "For Christ's sake, I forgive you!" After being obedient she sensed the filling of the Holy Spirit and felt only great love for her former enemy. [85]

THE POWER OF KINDNESS (4:4-6)

We see God's kindness to Jonah is rooted in his kindness to Israel and to all mankind. His kindness is all of grace. There is no merit involved.

God's Kindness to Israel

Jonah 4:2b | I knew that you are a gracious God and merciful, slow to anger and abounding in steadfast love, and relenting from disaster.

---

[85] Carole C. Carlson. *Corrie Ten Boom: Her Life, Her Faith: A Biography.* (Old Tappan, NJ: F.H. Revell, 1983) 78.

The irony here is that Israel had far more light than Nineveh (the capital of the Assyrian empire) but repented with so little of a message and no promise of redemption, even though God spared them. Yet Israel had so much light and revelation from God and were hardened. Why did God choose Israel? God tells us in Deuteronomy.

> *Deuteronomy 7:7-8* | It was not because you were more in number than any other people that the Lord set his love on you and chose you, for you were the fewest of all peoples, [8] but it is because the Lord loves you and is keeping the oath that he swore to your fathers, that the Lord has brought you out with a mighty hand and redeemed you from the house of slavery, from the hand of Pharaoh king of Egypt.

God's election of any sinner is unconditional. It's "not by works" or merit. Otherwise, we would have reason to boast (Eph 2:9). God loves us not because we are so great, but despite our rebellion which is hell deserving. The ground is level at the cross. Jonah doesn't deserve salvation any more than the Ninevites. We are all just as deserving of hell as unworthy of heaven as the most wicked and cruel Assyrian soldier. The ground is level at the cross. Jonah didn't get how undeserving he was of the steadfast love of God. He wanted it all to himself. "Keep those nasty Ninevites out of the kingdom," he must have thought!

God's Kind Nature

Jonah is stewing over this heaven-sent revival. We scratch out heads. Really? God asks Jonah about his anger, but we hear of no answer.

Jonah 4:4 | And the LORD said, "Do you do well to be angry?"

We don't see a response from Jonah about the people, but Jonah answers God later when his little plant withers, and God asks him the same question.

Jonah 4:9b | "Yes, I do well to be angry, angry enough to die."

At this point of the story, we rightly ask ourselves, "What is wrong with Jonah?" He should have been happy for the repentance of the Ninevites, but instead he is unhappy. He had been instrumental in the gift of spiritual life to thousands, but now he prefers death. He claimed to be cognizant of God's grace and mercy, which he himself had experienced. He resents God for it and says that he would have preferred wrath for Nineveh. One thing wrong with Jonah is that he is not understanding of the miracle of God's grace and love.[86]

Here's what God tells Jonah through his question. God is the one who has the true right to be angry! Grace is a miracle. In other words, the regeneration of sinners is an act of almighty God (cf Eph 2; Eze 36, 37). God has to do the work. God has to raise the dead. God has to give the increase (1 Cor 3:6). Just as God makes a plant grow to give the weary Jonah rest, he gives the increase so that a wretched sinner can be born again. Everything you have is a gift. That's grace!

God's Kindness to Jonah

Jonah doesn't answer God as to why he is angry about the revival in Nineveh, but he instead goes out and gets some rest in a little room he builds, kind of like the temporary shelters they would have quickly constructed in Israel during the Feast of Tabernacles. God wants to help him with his rest, and God in his kindness, he grows a sheltered vine to give Jonah shade and rest.

> **Jonah 4:5-6** | Jonah went out of the city and sat to the east of the city and made a booth for himself there. He sat under it in the shade, till he should see what would become of the city. **6** Now the LORD God appointed a plant and made it come up over Jonah, that it might be a shade over his head, to save him from his discomfort. So Jonah was exceedingly glad because of the plant.

The contrast here between God's heart and Jonah's is striking. God cares about Jonah's temporal comfort, but Jonah doesn't care about the Ninevites eternal comfort. Some have wondered what kind of plant it was the grew up over Jonah. Horticulturists have determined that it was a castor oil shrub which would have been "a lush, fast-growing provider of shade."[87] It is can quickly reach the size of a small tree, up to thirty-nine feet. It's long leaves (up to 20 inches long) would have provided ample shade for Jonah.

Here we see the long-suffering heart of God. God loves the wicked Assyrians. But God also loves the hard-hearted, smug, self-righteous, and at times racist prophet, Jonah.

---

[86] Boice, *Minor Prophets*, 305.

[87] Jules Janick and Harry S. Paris, "Jonah and the Gourd at Nineveh: Consequences of a Classic Mistranslation" *Cucurbitaceae Conference 2006* (Lafayette, IN: Purdue University, 2006), 349-357. https://hort.purdue.edu/newcrop/jonah.pdf

THE PROBLEM OF IDOLATRY (4:5-11)

Why is Jonah such a bad missionary? He's likely the worst ever. His problem is that he's going to reach idol worshippers, but we find out he's in need of rescue just as much as the Ninevites.

What's at the root of this? It's idolatry. Jonah goes to Nineveh to condemn idolatry, but who is the real idol worshipper in our story? An idol is anything that takes the place of God. Jonah loves his castor oil tree more than the people of Nineveh. Jonah loves himself. The central motive for all idolatry is the flesh: the self-life.

Jonah 4:5-11 | Jonah went out of the city and sat to the east of the city and made a booth for himself there. He sat under it in the shade, till he should see what would become of the city. [6] Now the LORD God appointed a plant and made it come up over Jonah, that it might be a shade over his head, to save him from his discomfort. So Jonah was exceedingly glad because of the plant. [7] But when dawn came up the next day, God appointed a worm that attacked the plant, so that it withered. [8] When the sun rose, God appointed a scorching east wind, and the sun beat down on the head of Jonah so that he was faint. And he asked that he might die and said, "It is better for me to die than to live." [9] But God said to Jonah, "Do you do well to be angry for the plant?" And he said, "Yes, I do well to be angry, angry enough to die." [10] And the LORD said, "You pity the plant, for which you did not labor, nor did you make it grow, which came into being in a night and perished in a night. [11] And should not I pity Nineveh, that great city, in which there are more than 120,000 persons who do not know their right hand from their left, and also much cattle?"

These are some of the strangest verses in the Bible upon first read. But as you think about them, they become incredibly convicting. You've got to remember where Jonah has come from great prosperity to really appreciate these verses. Jonah comes from green Galilee in Israel during the prosperous and enriched reign of Jeroboam II. His entitlement attitude when it comes to earthly comfort is frighteningly blinding. The idol of earthly comfort put blinders on the eyes of the prophet Jonah.

The Wait: the Apathy of Earthly Comfort

Earthly comfort and materialism can lull us to sleep. It makes Jonah think he's better than the Ninevites. He makes a booth and just passively waits for God to judge Nineveh.

Jonah 4:5 | Jonah went out of the city and sat to the east of the city and made a booth for himself there. He sat under it in the shade, till he should see what would become of the city.

There is Jonah waiting, like a person who has staked out a good view of the fireworks show. It seems Jonah is convinced he's going to see a real pyrotechnics display, a new Sodom and Gomorrah. God is holy right? He must destroy them! What apathy he has. We read of no praying, no pleading for God to have mercy. Jonah had heard the wailing in the streets. He had seen the great and mighty King Assurdan II pitiful state as he sat in ashes with tears streaming down his face. The site of thousands sitting in sackcloth and ashes was imprinted on Jonah's mind. Could it have been real humility, real repentance? No! How could it be? These were dogs! They have to burn! They must have previously heard of Yahweh's covenant love for Israel, delivering from the greatest army in the ancient world. They heard of this great God who split the Red Sea. But had these people truly trusted in the one true Almighty God? Sadly, and shockingly, he's hoping not. He wants them to burn.

Jonah's there in his nice booth, with his shade tree. He could care less about these precious souls. He's waiting, completely apathetic about the Ninevites eternity. He doesn't care if they perish.

The Weed: the Appearance of Earthly Comfort

Jonah was a man accustomed to earthly comfort. Where we live, earthly comfort is everywhere. God relieves Jonah's temporal discomfort by growing him a plant, a castor oil plant to be precise. It's like a big leafy plant that can grow overnight, and at times is the size of a small tree.

Jonah 4:6 | Now the LORD God appointed a plant and made it come up over Jonah, that it might be a shade over his head, to save him from his discomfort. So Jonah was exceedingly glad because of the plant.

God loves Jonah and takes care of him, even in his sinful bitterness. It is hot where Jonah sits—hot enough that the makeshift booth cannot provide enough shade. So the Lord appoints a plant with large leaves to grow up over Jonah to give him more shade—in one day's time no less (which itself is mercy). The story reveals that the Lord gives this provision to save him from his discomfort, or literally, to "rescue" him from his "evil" or "trouble."[88] Jonah, the text says, "was exceedingly glad because of the plant." Maybe he's a little too glad.

Remember, the time of Jonah in northern Israel was one of unprecedented prosperity. Jeroboam II had continued the ultimate prosperity religion: Baal worship. Jonah surely preached against Baal worship, but certainly enjoyed the prosperity a little too much.

Jonah would have preferred that the city be overthrown, but through his prophecy the city repented and was spared by the Lord, much to Jonah's dismay. Jonah is infected with chronic comfort-zone-itis. He's got it bad. He loves the comfort of his little booth and his castor oil plant. He just loves it. How much does he love his earthly comfort and security? When it's taken away, he wants to die!

How about you? Do you realize the suffocating nature of materialism? God's good gifts are precious and wonderful, but they are never to be put in the place of God. Our wealth, our comfort, our family, our home, our children—should never take the place of God. God must be at the center. Everything, even the best of our relationships, is rubbish compared to knowing Christ.

The Worm: the Atrophy of Earthly Comfort

The problem with anything on earth is that it is temporal. It cannot be trusted in. It atrophies and withers and dies.

Jonah 4:7 | But when dawn came up the next day, God appointed a worm that attacked the plant, so that it withered.

Oh, that dreaded worm! A little worm can take away Jonah's happiness. This demonstrates that foothold of idolatry in the heart of Jonah. He had put his happiness in something that can be taken away. What's your castor oil plant that can be taken away so easily?

---

[88] Eric Redmond, William Curtis, and Ken Fentress, *Exalting Jesus in Jonah, Micah, Nahum, Habakkuk* (Nashville, TN: Holman Reference, 2016), 56.

We see that once Jonah was rested and cared for by God, the Lord allowed the castor oil plant to die. Jonah turned God's mercy to him into an idol. You can turn the good gifts of God into idols.

We can all turn our comfort zone into a false savior, like Jonah did. God killing the castor oil plant was unveiling the lingering idols of comfort in the heart of Jonah. The Lord sent a scorching wind to prepare Jonah and us for this convicting lesson. Jonah was so singed by the sun that the Bible says he was ready to faint. Jonah pitied the plant more than the people of Nineveh. He had his booth and shade. When that was taken away from him, he told the God he was supposed to be serving, basically: "Let the world go to hell as long as I have my little place of comfort." He was out of northern Israel, but northern Israel and its prosperity religions still had hold of his heart. What an indictment! Consider the power of earthly comfort. Jonah was so embittered by the loss of his precious little plant, that he would rather die. He cared so much more about his plant than the 120,000 immortal souls of the Ninevite children and their parents.

So what's your plant? That castor oil plant grew up so quick and provided needed shade. Before we judge Jonah too harshly, let's remember he had been dowsed with the stomach contents of the great fish. He had walked a day's journey into the greater Nineveh area into the city. He had seen the greatest revival in a pagan land in the entire Old Testament. Exhaustion can bring us to a place of being irrational. Remember the great prophet Elijah's plea under a different place of shade. He collapsed under his broom tree and wanted to die.

1 Kings 19:4b | He asked that he might die, saying, "It is enough; now, O Lord, take away my life, for I am no better than my fathers."

Elijah had his broom tree. Jonah had his castor oil plant. Both provided plenty of shade and a place of rest. But what if God, as he did with Jonah, chooses to take away your plant with a worm? What is it that causes you to lose sight of the precious souls God has given you and sulk with anger, wanting to die if it is taken away? What do you have more pity for than the precious souls around you?

The Wind: the Amputation of Earthly Comfort

We may not appreciate God's amputation of our idols at first, but truly "the Lord gives and the Lord takes away," and we can say "blessed be the name of the Lord" (Job 1:20).

Jonah 4:8 | When the sun rose, God appointed a scorching east
wind, and the sun beat down on the head of Jonah so that he was
faint. And he asked that he might die and said, "It is better for me
to die than to live."

Realize, when god takes away your castor oil plant, he's not mad at
you. He loves you. He just wants you to worship him, not the plant!

After all Jonah's chastening, he still has an idolatry problem. Even
after his ssecond chance, the idolatry of his heart comes right back to
bite him. How we react to the loss of anything reveals who or what we
are really trusting in. Take Job for example. His kids, his home and
eventually his health are all taken away. But look at the most brutal
moment when his kids are taken. What is Job's response? Worship. He
thanks God for his good gifts and worships the Lord.

Jonah demonstrates that when we walk in the flesh, we are capable
of incredible irrational thinking. Bitterness makes us stupid. Jonah
thought he had a reason for anger. It's just not fair. God your grace is
good enough to save good sinners. That was Jonah's narrow theology.
Believe this false theology is alive and well. It is hurting the church of
Jesus. The truth is, God's grace is not just good enough for good sinners, but for the worst of sinners. In other words, grace is not about
what's fair. If we want fairness, then we all go to hell. Grace is outside
the realm of God's justice. It's in the realm of mercy.

The Whining: the Addiction to Earthly Comfort

Jonah 4:9 | But God said to Jonah, "Do you do well to be angry for the
plant?" And he said, "Yes, I do well to be angry, angry enough to
die."

The truth is the fountain of Jonah's anger is entitlement. It's not
fair! He thinks he's better. He thinks he's owed a bit of comfort after all
he's been through! Let's all realize we are all Jonah, living in North
America in the twenty first century. We have unprecedented prosperity. The poor among us are richer than any king of the great kings of the
ancient world. We have far more prosperity than Jonah or the greatest
kings could have ever fathomed.

We are not too different than Jonah who loves a plant far more
than the people of Israel. So it is with us: we love our A/C sometimes
more than the souls of those perishing around us. We love comfort
more than conversion. However you want to say it, we are all a lot more

like Jonah than we'd like to admit. What's your plant? What is it that takes your heart away from loving the people God loves? Where do you go when you are hurting? That tells you everything you need to know about what you worship. Sadly, Jonah at times worshipped his comfort more than he cared about God's plan and people. All that time in the belly of the fish, and Jonah was still addicted to comfort. I hope he got help after chapter 4 ended! There is help for all of us. Start with Ephesians 4:22-24 and put off the old life and put on the new. Choose to walk in the Spirit at all times, and you will not fulfill the desires and compulsions of the flesh (Gal 5:16). Take advantage of fellowship and accountability in your local church (Eph 4:15b-16; Heb 10:24-25). True happiness and peace comes from living life the way God designed it, practicing the presence of God. There is only one way out of addiction. That is to discover the explosive power of a greater affection, namely loving God. David speaks of it in Psalm 63.

> *Psalm 63:3* | Because your steadfast love is better than life, my lips will praise you.

David could have taught Jonah a powerful lesson—a lesson we all need to learn today. We were all created for worship. If you don't worship him, you'll worship something or someone else. You could be addicted to porn or to power. You could be addicted to food or be co-dependent on a relationship, thinking a human being is your savior. You could be someone to the idolatry of alcohol or marijuana. You may be addicted to sex and adultery. And you'll never be set free until you know the affection for Christ that expels the power of your old addiction. All pleasure is a tattered and dull picture of true pleasure in Christ. Until you find out that Christ's unrelenting love is better than anything this life can offer, you cannot and will not be free. But once the Son of God sets you free, through the explosive power of his love, you will be free indeed.

You are I the place where Jonah was. Be careful not to be lulled into spiritual lukewarmness through the opioid of materialistic comfort. A good test of whether or not you worship the idol of earthly comfort is to consider your love and effort to reach the lost for Christ. Jonah was shackled by his own glib self-righteousness. Are you more upset when you lose a parking space or there's a shortage on toilet paper or ice cream or cars than you are with eternal souls around you? Oh how very much like Jonah we may be. Let us repent and renew our efforts to let God's heart take hold of us for the outcasts.

The Word: the Assurance of Ultimate Comfort

Instead of the expected fireball from above, Jonah heard a gentle voice. God addresses the idolatry of his heart directly. It's actually the voice of ultimate comfort. We serve a God who saves the worst of sinners! Hallelujah.

> **Jonah 4:10-11** | And the LORD said, "You pity the plant, for which you did not labor, nor did you make it grow, which came into being in a night and perished in a night. [11] And should not I pity Nineveh, that great city, in which there are more than 120,000 persons who do not know their right hand from their left, and also much cattle?"

God challenges Jonah to trust in the God of the castor oil tree. He's challenging Jonah to have a heart of compassion like himself. God loves the little children who don't know their right hand from their left. God even loves the animals. But Jonah, he loves himself. He loves his comfort. He loves his plant and his booth. He loves his home in Israel. We end the story with Jonah angry and entitled. Jonah is angry that the Ninevites have not perished, but that the castor oil tree did perish. He's glad to sacrifice the eternal on the altar of his immediate comfort.

Where is real comfort and ultimate happiness found? We are left hanging, aren't we? But it's right there in front of us. The God who loved the pagan sailors and the cruel Ninevites also loves hardened, self-righteous, respectable sinners like us! Sometimes we pity the loss of our electricity or internet more than we pity the perishing of souls. Something is wrong with us.

Conclusion

Jonah had far more spiritual light than the Assyrians. He thought he was too good to bring a message from God to the Assyrian Ninevites. What he didn't understand was that God was showing his patience just as much with Jonah as the Ninevites. Jonah is a filthy rotten sinner worthy of hell, just like the Assyrians. You would think after being miraculously given a second chance after near death in the belly of a fish, Jonah would be more humble and in line with God's will. Jonah was given just as much grace and mercy as the pagan Ninevites.

It reminds me of the story I read recently about a troubled little girl named Abigail. She had been adopted but had acted up so much that the previous family pulled out of the adoption. Another family, a Christian family, decided to adopt her. They gladly welcomed this new daughter, with all her scars and hurts, into their family.

One detail that came out was that for one reason or another, whenever Abigail's previous family vacationed at Disney World, they took their biological children with them, but they left Abigail with a family friend. Abby was just too much! When her new family announced that they were going to Disney World, they had no idea that Abby had a very bad trigger, so, thinking she could never be good enough to go, she started acting up more than normal. She caused so much trouble.

A couple of days before the family headed to Florida, the father pulled his newly adopted daughter into his lap to talk through her escapades. "I know what you're going to do," Abigail stated flatly. "You're not going to take me to Disney World, are you?"

The father asked her, "Is this trip something we're doing as a family?"

She nodded yes, brown eyes wide, rimming with tears.

"Are you part of this family?"

She nodded yes again.

"Then you're going with us —you're part of our family, and we're not leaving you behind."

"So Daddy, I'm going to Disney World, not because I am good but because I'm yours." [89]

It not because I'm good but because I'm yours. Why do we get to belong to the Lord? Why did Jonah belong to the Lord? Because he was good? No! Because God is good! We were bought with a high price.

That's the message of outrageous grace. That's the message of Jonah. Jonah did nothing to earn God's favor. Neither did the Ninevites. It's all of grace, such deep, deep grace. We don't get what we deserve. Christ bore that penalty for our sins. We are not good. Christ is good. He gets all the glory. We are saved not because we are good, but because in love he chose us and loved us. If you think of it that way, there's really no difference between Jonah and the Ninevites. And there's no difference between you and the people with hardest hearts.

---

[89] Daniel Montgomery, *Proof: Finding Freedom through the Intoxicating Joy of Irresistible Grace* (Grand Rapids, MI: Zondervan, 2014), 81-84.

Imagine, one day, when his life is over, Jonah enters heaven, more humble and wiser, hands raised in praise to God, together with the Ninevites and the pagan sailors. That's grace. None of us deserve that grace. Jonah may have been the worst missionary in history, but he still had an amazing harvest. Some plant. Some water. But God always, always, always gives the increase! Let's give praise to God for the book of Jonah because it's a powerful reminder that we are all in need of grace, especially those who know God and his word the most.

6 | JONAH 1:17

THE SIGN OF JONAH

Just as Jonah was three days and three nights in the belly of the great fish, so will the Son of Man be three days and three nights in the heart of the earth. The men of Nineveh will rise up at the judgment with this generation and condemn it, for they repented at the preaching of Jonah, and behold, something greater than Jonah is here.
MATTHEW 12:40-41

I have never been a miracle seeking Christian. Though I came to Christ in a Pentecostal environment with the Assemblies of God, I have always been a bit befuddled when people would talk about miracles, healings, visions, and dreams. That is until I met Dr. Ahmed Joktan. He was 26 when I met him. An accomplished medical doctor already at such a young age. Did I mention he grew up in Mecca, Saudi Arabia, birthplace of everything ISIS and terrorism and jihad? If there is a people that mirror the Assyrians of the ancient world, it is the jihadists of Islam. This young man grew up being trained in the same terrorist training camps as five of the 9/11 hijackers. Five of those hijackers are his cousins. God had saved him as a 19-year-old. It all began with a true miracle, a vision of the Lord Jesus Christ, who Muslims call "Isa." He was visiting New Zealand for a summer, learning English. Listen to his own testimony:

Sometime after drifting to sleep, I had a dream so vivid and real that I can see it even now as I write, playing before me as if on a movie screen. Cutting through the stillness of the night, the balcony doors of my room suddenly burst open and through the rushing wind came a booming, majestic voice, falling over me as a wave as deep and high and mighty as the sea itself. Then, like a magnificent fire of pure light, a glorious figure walked through the balcony doors toward me; so bright was his radiance that I could barely look upon it.

His voice was loud but also beautiful and inviting. He spoke to me in my mother tongue of Arabic.

"Come to me," he said.

This majestic, otherworldly figure was welcoming me and inviting me to come to him.

I was terrified. My heart beat uncontrollably beneath my chest. Fear took me from all sides. Trembling, I screamed the only words that came to mind, "Where must I go to find you?"

The figure, draped in a robe of sunlight, was so near, right before my eyes, yet so infinite and glorious that he both filled and extended far beyond what eyes could see. He seemed untouchable, so far away and yet so near and personal.

"Go to the house with white pillars," he answered. "There you shall find the truth."

I looked away, and there I saw that an entire side of the room had been transformed into the house of which he'd spoken, rising impossibly but in perfect alignment with the small space, keeping its true size and scope. And then, just as suddenly as it had begun, my dream ended.

Heart racing and clothes soaked, I awoke, drenched in wonder and terror. What had I just experienced? [90]

It wasn't long after that my Arabian friend found the house with white pillars, which was the "Baptist Tabernacle" of Auckland, New Zealand. There he found a pastor who had been praying and fasting for someone to come to Jesus from Saudi Arabia. Dr. Ahmed spoke with that pastor for three days, reading through the book of John in Arabic, and being born again when he came across Jesus' words in John 14.

---

[90] Ahmed Joktan, *From Mecca to Christ: A True Story from the Son of the Meccan Mufti* (Wenatchee, WA: Proclaim Publishers, 2020), 39-40.

John 14:6 | I am the way, and the truth, and the life. No one comes to the Father except through me.

With this, he entered the kingdom. The point is, even Dr. Ahmed, who was born and raised in a nation that makes reading the Bible a capital crime, had to come through the word of God, through the cross of Christ, to enter the kingdom. The greatest miracle, the greatest sign that can be given is the sign of the prophet Jonah. According to Jesus, for those seeking miracles, they need look no further than a hill called Calvary and to the empty tomb for the greatest miracle of all miracles. It's very similar to the miracle that happened to Jonah.

Jonah 1:17 | And the LORD appointed a great fish to swallow up Jonah. And Jonah was in the belly of the fish three days and three nights.

Three days and three nights. That sounds familiar. Jonah's experience is a prophetic picture—a foreshadowing, an acted-out prophecy—of what was to happen to the incarnate Son of God on the cross! Jonah went the way of death—so did Christ. Jonah remained for three days in the grip of death—so did Christ. Jonah returned to the land of the living on the third day—so did Christ. Jonah was a sign to the Ninevites and so was Christ a sign to his own and succeeding generations as one risen from the dead to be the author of eternal salvation to all who obey him. [91] Calvin correctly observes, "This deliverance of Jonah is an image of the resurrection."[92]

Matthew 12:38-41 | Then some of the scribes and Pharisees answered him, saying, "Teacher, we wish to see a sign from you." [39] But he answered them, "An evil and adulterous generation seeks for a sign, but no sign will be given to it except the sign of the prophet Jonah. [40] For just as Jonah was three days and three nights in the belly of the great fish, so will the Son of Man be three days and three nights in the heart of the earth. [41] The men of Nineveh will rise up at the judgment with this generation and condemn it, for they repented at the preaching of Jonah, and behold, something greater than Jonah is here.

---

[91] Gordon J. Keddie, *Preacher on the Run: The Meaning of Jonah*, Welwyn Commentary Series (Darlington, England: Evangelical Press, 1986), 70–71.

[92] John Calvin and John Owen, *Commentaries on the Twelve Minor Prophets*, vol. 3 (Bellingham, WA: Logos Bible Software, 2010), 91.

THE PLEA FOR A MIRACLE (MT 12:38)

Matthew 12:38 | Then some of the scribes and Pharisees answered
him, saying, "Teacher, we wish to see a sign from you."

Some people will blame their unbelief on the lack of a miracle. They
demand a miracle before they will believe. We must realize that miracles are not enough. The human heart is so hard, that outside of getting
a new heart, we will not believe. The Pharisees had just seen one of the
greatest miracles ever performed – a blind and deaf man was healed.
He could speak with reason; he could sing; he could now carry on an
intelligent conversation; he could now see and discern the faces of people. It was a display of miraculous power from our Lord. One who was
like a caged animal was now in his right mind.

The Pharisees have the audacity to ask for another miracle. They
want just a little bit more. The truth is miracles alone will not convince
anyone to follow Jesus Christ. Their rebellion must be cured. Miracles
cannot cure the rebel heart of man.

Perhaps you remember the story of the rich man and the beggar
Lazarus. The rich man ended up in hell and asked Father Abraham if
the beggar could go and warn his brothers? Jesus tells the rich man that
miracle can't help bring anyone to faith in the Lord. Only the Scriptures
can do that.

> *Luke 16:27-31* | I beg you, father, to send him to my father's
> house— 28 for I have five brothers—so that he may warn them, lest
> they also come into this place of torment.' 29 But Abraham said, 'They
> have Moses and the Prophets; let them hear them.' 30 And he said,
> 'No, father Abraham, but if someone goes to them from the dead, they
> will repent.' 31 He said to him, 'If they do not hear Moses and the
> Prophets, neither will they be convinced if someone should rise from
> the dead.

The word of God is more powerful than miracles. Miracles may not
engender faith, but the word of God will! Romans 10:17, "Faith comes
from hearing, and hearing through the word of Christ." The Pharisees
had so many high and holy privileges. First and foremost, they had the
oracles of God. They had the Bible of their time, the Old Testament.
They saw the miracles. They had the Messiah, the King who would subject all other kings in their midst. The kingdom of God had truly come

to them. Not only that, but this great King of kings also humbled himself and did signs and wonders in their midst. The blind saw, the deaf could hear, the lame could leap, the dead were now living. The Messiah had arrived. Yet they would not believe him for his word or even for the very miracles he did! Their hearts were hardened. They could demand another miracle, but miracles are futile to change the human heart unless they are mixed with faith in the word of God.

The request of the scribes and Pharisees, said nearly 2,000 years ago, is an everyday, every-generation request. But even more than a request, it is an excuse. People want signs that God exists and that Jesus is Lord, but the truth is, unless they believe the word of God, they will perish. There is no sign great enough to convince the rebel heart of man to turn to Jesus. Except one. Yes, there is *one sign*.

THE PICTURE OF THE MIRACLE (MT 12:39-40)

The one sign that will cause men to believe is illustrated by the miracle of Jonah. Jesus called it "the sign of the prophet Jonah." Now, of course the leaders of Israel, at least on in the group of the Pharisees, believed in the Bible literally. They believed Jonah was swallowed by a great fish. Christians are less inclined to insist that the fish was a whale; neither the Old Testament Hebrew nor the New Testament Greek says "whale." It could have been something related to a whale or some kind of great sea creature that is extinct today. The references are only to "a great fish." Nevertheless, those who adhere to the total trustworthiness of the Bible, now as then, rightly insist that Jonah was literally swallowed and was thus preserved alive for three days by the fish's action. To those who believe in the literal bodily resurrection of Jesus Christ, such an event is not at all impossible. Moreover, there is a direct connection between the two.[93] When unbelieving scribes and Pharisees asked Jesus for a miracle that might substantiate his extraordinary claims, Jesus told them of the miracle of Jonah as an illustration that would point to the ultimate miracle: Christ's resurrection from the dead.

Matthew 12:39-40 | But he answered them, "An evil and adulterous generation seeks for a sign, but no sign will be given to it except the sign of the prophet Jonah. **40** For just as Jonah was three days

---

[93] Boice, *The Minor Prophets*, 262.

and three nights in the belly of the great fish, so will the Son of
Man be three days and three nights in the heart of the earth.

So here we see a great foreshadowing in Jonah to the death, burial,
and resurrection of Christ.

The Picture of Jesus' Death

"The sign of the prophet Jonah" points to Jesus' death. Jonah's
watery grave points to the death of Jesus. Just as Jonah was "as good
as dead" for three days in the belly of the fish and then came alive again,
so Christ was truly dead and came alive after three days. Like all mankind, Jonah deserved to die. He was thrown into the Mediterranean Sea
and was as good as dead. When Scripture says that the wages of sin is
death (Rom 6:23), it lays down the most inescapable and irrefutable
absolute of human experience. Ten out of ten people die because every
single one is a sinner! This is why we die physically, and it is why the
unsaved die eternally. Jonah's consignment to a watery grave and his
incarceration in the fish meant that he was as good as dead. He was not
really dead, of course, but as far as he and the sailors knew, he was finished. He therefore was a most convincing proof of the wrath of God
against sin and the necessity of the satisfaction of divine justice in the
full punishment of sin!

Now, according to Christ himself, Jonah's death sentence prefig-
ures Christ's own death. It foreshadows what had to happen to Jesus in
order for God's wrath against human sin to be satisfied through an
atonement which could accomplish the salvation of the lost. Jonah's
death sentence is a picture of the death of Christ—that death which actually paid the sin-debt. By it, Jesus paid the penalty of sin (expiation),
placated the displeasure of God against the sinner (propitiation) and
restored believers to the favor and fellowship of God (reconciliation).
Jesus' death procures a new heart (regeneration), a new record (forgiveness) and a new future (eternal life) for all who will trust in him as
their Savior and Lord.

The Picture of Jesus' Burial

Just as Jonah was "buried" in the fish for three days and nights, so
our Lord was "buried" and raised on the third day. Don't be confused
at the three days, three nights reference. Jesus is comparing signs. Any
part of a day in the Jewish culture was accounted at an entire day.

Christ was crucified at 3pm on Friday. So you have Friday day and Friday night; Saturday day, and Saturday night, and then you have Sunday morning. It's considered an entire day.

Jonah's time in the belly of the great fish pictures Jesus as he went through the hell of Calvary and was three days in the heart of the earth for the sake of people like us. "Christ died for our sins according to the Scriptures ... he was buried ... he was raised on the third day" (1 Cor 15:3). "Christ died for sins once for all, the righteous for the unrighteous, to bring you to God" (1 Pet 3:18). Jonah's three days in the fish emphasized that the wages of sin is death and that, if anyone was ever to be forgiven the consequences of his sin, then there had to be an atonement sufficient to cover the need. In this sense, Jesus' death and burial was the 'sign of Jonah' for his own generation. The sign the Pharisees ought to have looked for was simply the death and resurrection of Christ.

The Picture of Jesus' Resurrection

Jesus referred to this entire experience of Jonah as a historical illustration that pictured his own literal resurrection, thus reinforcing the truthfulness of this narrative.[94] The point is the only sign that will convert people is the death, burial, and resurrection of Christ. Nothing else will work. You could have entire cemeteries made alive and whole, and if you sent them on evangelism, no one would believe unless God worked in their hearts.

After three days, Jonah was cast up on the beach. He came back, as it were, from the dead. He was saved to serve God another day. The experience prepared him, in his own heart, to fulfil his former calling to preach the word of God to Nineveh. But it had its effect on his hearers when in due course he did preach to them. It was a means of bringing these Gentiles to God in a most dramatic way, for Jonah was a sign to Nineveh (Lk 11:30). Can you imagine, as Jonah preached to the king? To his surprise, the king was eager to listen. We already mentioned, and as history records, the king had previously experienced God's calling and drawing in his life. And here is this prophet returning from his watery grave, resurrected to talk to the king about the God he was already being drawn to. Jonah's return from the sea was a resurrection that authenticated his message and was the chosen channel of God's

---

[94] Ibid.

power that changed the heart attitudes of these people. That explains why the message of God's wrath had the effect of being a message of life! Instead of being turned off or offended, or perhaps even amused, they are brought to living faith!

God's message can transform even the hardest of human hearts. It is sharper than any double-edged sword, and it will divide "soul and spirit, joints and marrow." It judges "the thoughts and attitudes of the heart" (Heb 4:12). And so with Jonah and the Ninevites, the conjunction of the hard message and the sign of his resurrection persuades them that God is gracious and is willing to give life to needy, lost, hurting people who apply to him for mercy.

To the Jews of Jesus' day, the 'sign of Jonah' would be reissued in the resurrection of Jesus. He would rise from the dead, to be declared throughout the world as the only Savior for mankind. Remember what Peter told the Jewish leaders after Pentecost?

> *Acts 4:12* | Salvation is found in no one else, for there is no other name under heaven given to men by which we must be saved.

The "sign of Jonah" forever points to Christ dying for sinners in their place and rising in victory over sin and death for their justification (Rom 4:25). Hugh Martin summarizes it well:

> For us, he bare the wrath of God; and just as in his favor is life; so in the wrath of God is death. For us, all the days of his flesh, he was made sin; and the wages of sin is death. But he died the death to an end— he died it all—he died it out. He died death dead and done. [95]

As Jonah stood alive on the shores of Nineveh, so Jesus stood alive on the shores of Galilee.

Contrasts with Jesus

The contrast between Jonah and Christ is drawn to demonstrate that while Jonah is the type of Christ, Jesus is the fulfillment.

A Greater Message

Matthew 12:41a | The men of Nineveh will rise up at the judgment with this generation and condemn it, for they repented at the preaching of Jonah.

---

[95] Hugh Martin, *The Prophet Jonah: His Character and Mission to Nineveh* (London: Alexander Strahan Publishers, 1866), 288.

The men of Nineveh repented at a lesser message and through a lesser messenger. That's why the Pharisees are so condemned. They have far more light than the pagan Ninevites, yet they give far more resistance to the good news of God's mercy.

"Repent for your city will be destroyed in forty days" is a far dimmer message than, "Repent and believe the good news that the Messiah has arrived and would have your allegiance."

A Greater Messenger

Matthew 12:41b | Behold, something greater than Jonah is here.

The whole doctrine of the person and work of Christ is comprehended in this expression. Jesus was perfect in his humanity. Jonah though a child of God, was one, like all of us, had broken God's law—like Adam, of the dust of the earth, a sinner who could not save himself, though a believer and a prophet of God. Jonah was thrown to his "death" because he was guilty. Jesus was put to death as the sinless Son of God. Jonah as prophet was a mediator, pointing to the ultimate Mediator. Jesus as mediator came, the sinless Son of man, the enfleshed Son of God, *the* Prophet, Priest and King. He was the only begotten of the Father, full of grace and truth. He was "the last Adam," a life-giving spirit and the Lord of glory who would be crucified for the sins of the world, willingly and lovingly laying down his life for his enemies that he might give them eternal life and bring them into a saving relationship with himself. His birth, life and ministry all pointed to his being the promised Messiah, the Lamb of God who would take away the sin of the world. However amazing the "resurrection" of Jonah was, it was a faded black and white photo compared to the Messiah, in living color, alive and victorious, rising from the dead. and however revealing of the grace of God the sign of Jonah, all is but the palest shadow of the revelation of God in the person and work of Christ, for he is "the propitiation for our sins, and not only for ours but also for the sins of the whole world" (1 Jn 2:2).

THE PRIORITY OF THE MIRACLE (MT 12:41A)

Since the Pharisees have a greater message from a greater Messenger, they will be held accountable to a higher standard. They were given the "pearl of great price"—an invitation to know and love Christ, and they passed it up. They said, "No thank you." "To whom much is given,

much will be required" (Lk 12:48). They had more privilege than any
generation before them, more light, more of God's word, but they chose
to reject God's greatest gift. They chose to make no priority out of what
should have been their greatest priority. To make this point, Jesus calls
the well-saved Ninevites in heaven as witnesses against the hard-
hearted Pharisees. The Gentiles here are called to testify against these
Jewish leaders.

> **Matthew 12:41a** | The men of Nineveh will rise up at the judgment
> with this generation and condemn it, for they repented at the
> preaching of Jonah.

The Ninevites' Response

It will not be the Jews who will condemn these Gentile Ninevites in
the Judgement Day, as the Jews liked to think. The reverse will be the
case. They had an inferior message from an inferior prophet, but they
repented. The Jews had all the privileges and the promises, but they
rejected the enfleshed Word himself (Jn 1:14). Their response to the
Word—the Scriptures and the Logos, Jesus Christ—would determine
their eternal destiny. And the utter waste of their covenant privileges,
in their apostasy from the Lord, will be forever set against the repentance of the Ninevites.

Those with great light will be held to account. Jesus makes the
point more strikingly by looking ahead to the day of judgment. The
leaders of Jesus' day rejected the message of repentance and faith, but
the pagan Ninevites accepted it and turned to God. Jesus says, "These
pagan Ninevites were less enlightened than you, but they repented. You
have far more enlightenment than they ever had."

The Pharisees' Resistance

On the other hand, the Jews stood against Christ, even to the point
of nailing him to a cross. They had all the privileges; they were the covenant people of God; they had the Scriptures and, most significantly of
all, they had the Lord Jesus Christ among them, fulfilling the promises
of the word of God and revealing himself as the Savior of sinners. The
eternal love of God was being poured out before them in the only-be-
gotten Son. Yet they despised and rejected him. They crucified the Lord
of glory. "He came unto his own, and his own did not receive him" (Jn
1:11).

Your Response

Christians today sometimes feel that "if only Jesus were here" then people would be more ready to listen to the gospel message. They know, of course, that he is not going to come until the great day when Jesus returns. But they imagine themselves in the position and privilege that the people of Jesus' time had when they could hear him explain God's word and perform miracles of healing. But the truth is that people were *not* more willing to commit themselves to Christ when they could see him with their own eyes and hear him with their own ears. Seeing is not the same as believing! In fact, the people he grew up among were the very people who were quickest to reject him (Mt 13:53–58). In the story of the rich man and Lazarus the beggar, Jesus told how the rich man, in hell, asked that Lazarus be sent from heaven to warn his five brothers, so that they would repent. Abraham answered, 'They have Moses and the Prophets; let them listen to them.' In other words, they should read their Bibles—they should listen to what God had said in black and white (Lk 16:19–31).

All that the Ninevites had was a heathen background, a prophet who was not only a restored backslider but a foreigner and a message that was all doom and gloom. A preacher like that in such a situation today might be expected to raise a few laughs, even assuming that anyone bothered to give him a hearing. But Nineveh repented!

What's your response to Jesus? It is simple faith alone that saves. The Pharisees had Bible knowledge, but that does no good for people with proud hearts. They had power, riches, intelligence, and luxury. The Pharisees came to God with their hands full, trying to merit salvation. They were blinded by all their religious idolatry and self-righteousness. The Ninevites came with nothing but sackcloth and ashes. As Toplady's hymn goes, "Nothing in my hand I bring, only to thy cross I cling."

If a saving relationship with God were based on human strength, then only those who could bench-press at least 300 pounds would get into Heaven. If it was based on human intelligence, "getting into heaven would be like getting into Harvard," and only a very few elite academics could do it. If it were based on beauty, only a few people like my wife would experience divine glory. But if salvation is obtained by grace alone through faith alone, then even humble folk like fishermen and weak people like little children can gain entrance into the kingdom of heaven. Faith allows all kinds of people (strong/weak, pretty/ugly, smart/dumb, black/white, male/female, Jew/Gentile, and so on) to enter the kingdom.

THE PROVIDER OF THE MIRACLE (MT 12:41B)

Matthew 12:41b | And behold, something greater than Jonah is here.

Look no further. Jesus is here and ready to save you. Christ has already come. God in human flesh. Behold him. He's greater than the-prophets and priests of the Old Testament. He's greater than the apostles of the New Testament. He's greater than angels. His message is greater than dreams and visions. He offers you something no one can offer you: eternal life. I can't save you. Jonah can't save you. But Jesus can save you!

Dear friend, you and I will be held to a greater account than the people of Nineveh. We celebrate the King of kings at Christmas and Easter. Our very calendars refer to him with A.D. (in the year of our Lord). But I'm asking you to know him personally. The greatest prophet has arrived – greater than Jonah. Greater than Elijah. The greatest King has arrived. Someone greater, wiser and more powerful and more renowned than Solomon. Here is the Son of God bidding you to come to him and trust him for eternal life. He died for your sins. He rose again. Come to him and have your sins all forgiven. Be adopted into God's forever family.

The people of Nineveh repented and responded to the revealed message of the God of Israel. Jesus is the image of the invisible God. He's the ultimate message. What will you do with him? When the Lord said to the Jews, "For as Jonah was a sign to the Ninevites, so also will the Son of man be to this generation" (Lk 11:30), he was establishing the ultimate unspoken question for every generation. "What will you do with the sign of the Son of man?" Jonah's story is amazing, but behold, "something greater than Jonah is here." That something is a Someone. What will you do with the Christ who died and rose again on the third day? Will you, with Nineveh, repent and change your ways? Or will you, with the scribes and the Pharisees, despise and reject the good news of salvation in Jesus Christ?[96]

---

[96] Keddie, *Preacher on the Run*, 71–76.

Conclusion

I recently read about a California man who ran into a bear while texting. Sometimes we are so distracted, we miss the obvious. Jesus is manifested before us dear ones. The prophet Jonah points us to someone infinitely greater than Jonah. Jesus Christ is the great Prophet, but more than a prophet. He is the great King, but more than a king. He is the King of kings and the Lord of Lords. He is the God of the universe, the Lord of heaven and earth. Is he the master and controller of your life? He's worthy of your surrender and your praise. Jonah gave his life to save the sailors. He was in the belly of the fish three days and three nights. Jesus lived his perfect life and died a substitutionary death for you and was in the belly of the grave for us. What a miracle that Christ rose for us! Trust in him with all your heart. Serve him! Love him! We serve a risen Savior!

SELECTED BIBLIOGRAPHY

In order of appearance in the commentary

COMMENTARIES

Jay Sklar, "Jonah," in *Daniel–Malachi*, ed. Iain M. Duguid, James M. Hamilton Jr., and Jay Sklar, vol. VII, ESV Expository Commentary (Wheaton, IL: Crossway, 2018).

Carl Friedrich Keil and Franz Delitzsch, *Commentary on the Old Testament*, vol. 7 (Peabody, MA: Hendrickson, 1996).

Donald J. Wiseman, T. Desmond Alexander, and Bruce K. Waltke, *Obadiah, Jonah and Micah: An Introduction and Commentary*, vol. 26, Tyndale Old Testament Commentaries (Downers Grove, IL: InterVarsity Press, 1988).

Colin S. Smith, *Jonah: Navigating a God-centered Life* (Ross-shire, Scotland: Christian Focus Publications, 2012).

James E. Smith, *The Minor Prophets*, Old Testament Survey Series (Joplin, MO: College Press, 1994).

Leslie C. Allen, *The Books of Joel, Obadiah, Jonah, and Micah* (Grand Rapids, MI: Wm. B. Eerdmans, 1976).

James Bruckner, *Jonah, Nahum, Habakkuk, Zephaniah*, The NIV Application Commentary (Grand Rapids, MI: Zondervan Publishing House, 2004).

Timothy Keller, *Rediscovering Jonah: The Secret to God's Mercy* (New York: Penguin Publishing Group, 2018).

Duane A. Garrett, *Explore the Bible: Adult Commentary: Hosea, Amos, Jonah (Winter 2012–13): Revealing the Heart of God* (LifeWay Christian Resources, 2013).

Gordon J. Keddie, *Preacher on the Run: The Meaning of Jonah*, Welwyn Commentary Series (Darlington, England: Evangelical Press, 1986).

Rosa Ching Shao, *Jonah (Asia Bible Commentary Series)* (Langham Global Library, 2019).

William Banks, Jonah: *The Reluctant Prophet* (Chicago: Moody, 1966), 20.

Warren W. Wiersbe, *Be Amazed*, "Be" Commentary Series (Wheaton, IL: Victor Books, 1996).

James Limburg, *Jonah: A Commentary* (Louisville, KY: Westminster/Knox Press, 1993).

James A. Long, *Jonah: A Tale of Mercy* (Durham, NC: Torchflame Books / Light Messages, 2016).

Janet Howe Gaines, *Forgiveness in a Wounded World: Jonah's Dilemma* (Atlanta: Society of Biblical Literature, 2003).

Iain M. Duguid, *Jonah: Grace for Sinners and Saints* (New Growth Press, 2019).

David Watson, *Called & Committed* (Harold Shaw Publishers, Wheaton, IL; 1982).

Rod Mattoon, *Treasures from Jonah*, Treasures from Scripture Series (Springfield, IL: Rod Mattoon, 2003).

Richard D. Phillips, *Jonah & Micah*, ed. Richard D. Phillips, Philip Graham Ryken, and Iain M. Duguid, Reformed Expository Commentary (Phillipsburg, NJ: P&R Publishing, 2010).

James Montgomery Boice, *The Minor Prophets: An Expositional Commentary* (Grand Rapids, MI: Baker Books, 2002), 284, *cf* Frank Knight, *Nile and the Jordan* (London: James Clarke & Co., Ltd., 1921).

David Guzik, *Jonah*, David Guzik's Commentaries on the Bible (Santa Barbara, CA: David Guzik, 2000).

Kevin J. Youngblood, *Jonah*, ed. Daniel I. Block, Zondervan Exegetical Commentary on the Old Testament (Grand Rapids, MI: Zondervan, 2015).

Eric Redmond, William Curtis, and Ken Fentress, *Exalting Jesus in Jonah, Micah, Nahum, Habakkuk* (Nashville, TN: Holman Reference, 2016).

Douglas Stuart, "Jonah," in *New Bible Commentary: 21st Century Edition*, ed. D. A. Carson et al., 4th ed. (Leicester, England; Downers Grove, IL: Inter-Varsity Press, 1994).

Lawrence O. Richards, *The Teacher's Commentary* (Wheaton, IL: Victor Books, 1987).

SERMONS

Timothy J. Keller, *The Timothy Keller Sermon Archive* (New York City: Redeemer Presbyterian Church, 2013).

Charles Haddon Spurgeon. "Salvation is of the Lord" *The New Park Street Pulpit*, preached May 10, 1857 (London: Passemore and Alabaster, 1857).

ANCIENT SOURCES

Martin Luther in Mark Johnston, *Saving God: Religion After Idolatry*. Princeton, NJ: Princeton University Press, 2009).

John Calvin and John Owen, *Commentaries on the Twelve Minor Prophets*, vol. 3 (Bellingham, WA: Logos Bible Software, 2010).

BIOGRAPHICAL

David Matthews, *I Saw the Welsh Revival: An Account of the 1904 Revival in Wales* (Goshen, IN: Pioneer Books, 1992).

Dr. Ahmed Joktan, *From Mecca to Christ: A True Story from the Son of the Meccan Mufti* (Wenatchee, WA: Proclaim Publishers, 2020).

Iain Harnish Murray, *Revival and Revivalism: The Making and Marring of American Evangelicalism, 1750-1858* (Edinburgh etc.: Banner of Truth Trust, 1996).

Carole C. Carlson. *Corrie Ten Boom: Her Life, Her Faith: A Biography*. (Old Tappan, NJ: F.H. Revell, 1983).

William Young Fullerton, *Charles Haddon Spurgeon, A Biography* (London: Williams and Norgate Publishers, 1920).

COUNSELING

Robert D. Jones. *Pursuing Peace* (Wheaton: Crossway, 2012).

Jim Berg. *God is More than Enough* (Greenville, SC: BJU Press/Journey-Forth, 2010).

Erwin W. Lutzer, *When You've Been Wronged: Moving from Bitterness to Forgiveness* (Chicago, IL: Moody Publishers, 2007).

Daniel Montgomery, *Proof: Finding Freedom through the Intoxicating Joy of Irresistible Grace* (Grand Rapids, MI: Zondervan, 2014).

DICTIONARIES

James Strong, *Enhanced Strong's Lexicon* (Woodside Bible Fellowship, 1995).

Noah Webster, *Webster's Dictionary: An American Dictionary of the English Language*, 4th Edition (New York: S. Converse Publishing, 1828).

International Standard Bible Encyclopedia, "Nineveh" by T. G. Pinches.

Wycliffe Bible Encyclopedia, "Nineveh," by Elmer B. Smick.
The New Bible Dictionary, "Nineveh," by D. J. Wiseman.

BACKGROUNDS
Hugh Martin, *The Prophet Jonah: His Character and Mission to Nineveh*
    (London: Alexander Strahan Publishers, 1866).
Jules Janick and Harry S. Paris, "Jonah and the Gourd at Nineveh: Conse-
    quences of a Classic Mistranslation" *Cucurbitaceae Conference 2006*
    (Lafayette, IN: Purdue University, 2006), 349-357. https://hort.pur-
    due.edu/newcrop/jonah.pdf.
Joshua J. Mark, "The Neo-Assyrian Empire," *World History Encyclopedia*
    (Surrey,   UK: World   History   Publishing,   2014),
    https://www.worldhistory.org/Neo-Assyrian_Empire/.
Jonathan Reich, *Ancient Assyrians: History, Civilization & Culture* (Mountain
    View, CA: Study.com, 2022), https://study.com/academy/lesson/an-
    cient-assyrians-history-civilization-culture.html
Salvatore Gaspa, "Textiles in the Neo-Assyrian Empire," January 1, 2018,
    https://doi.org/10.1515/9781501503054.
M. Broshi, I. Finkelstein, (1992). "The Population of Palestine in Iron Age II",
    Bulletin of the American School of Oriental Research.
Heffron Yağmur et al., *At the Dawn of History Ancient Near Eastern Studies
    in Honor of J.N. Postgate* (Winona Lake, IN: Eisenbrauns, 2017).

THEOLOGY
Ambrose John Wilson, "The Sign of the Prophet Jonah and its Modern Con-
    firmations," *Princeton Theological Review, vol 25* (1927).
Daniel C. Timmer, *A Gracious and Compassionate God: Mission, Salvation
    and Spirituality in the Book of Jonah*, ed. D. A. Carson, vol. 26, New
    Studies in Biblical Theology (England; Downers Grove, IL: Apollos;
    InterVarsity Press, 2011).
Mark Allen Powell, "Echoes of Jonah in the New Testament" (Spring 2007),
    Luther Seminary Journal, Volume 27, No. 2.

TOPICAL
C.S. Lewis, *Miracles* (New York: Touchstone, 1996).
Dietrich Bonhoeffer, *Life Together* (Dietrich Bonhoeffer Works) (Minneap-
    olis, MN: Fortress Press, 2015).

Timothy Keller, *Counterfeit Gods: The Empty Promises of Money, Sex, and Power, and the Only Hope That Matters* (Riverhead Books, 2011).

Joni Eareckson Tada, "God Permits What He Hates," *International Disability Center* (Joni and Friends, January 31, 2014), http://registration.joni-andfriends.org/radio/4-minute/god-permits-what-he-hates2/.

Leonard Ravenhill in Timothy Hill, *Beyond the Mist: A Quest for Authentic Revival* (Branson, MO: Tim Hill Ministries, 2010).

Brian Chappell, "How to Illustrate", *Christ-Centered Preaching: Preparation & Delivery of Sermons*, (Covenant Theological Seminary, St. Louis, MO, Fall 2006), https://media.thegospelcoalition.org/wp-content/uploads/2017/11/10180057/CCP_T_Lecture_14A.pdf, Lecture 14A.

Martyn Lloyd-Jones, *Revival* (Wheaton, IL: Crossway, 1987).

PROCLAIM
PUBLISHERS

WENATCHEE, WASHINGTON

You may obtain this, and many other fine resources made
available by Proclaim Publishers by contacting us:

Web:
proclaimpublishers.com

Email:
contact@proclaimpublishers.com

Postal Mail:
Proclaim Publishers
PO Box 2082
Wenatchee, WA 98807

SOLI DEO GLORIA

www.ingramcontent.com/pod-product-compliance
Lightning Source LLC
Chambersburg PA
CBHW021930040426
42448CB00008B/995